WHEN IT COMES TO SPOONING, I'M A FORK

AND OTHER TALES FROM THE FRONT LINES OF MARRIAGE AND PARENTHOOD

MARC PREY

Contents

"Behind every great man is a woman rolling her eyes."

-Anonymous

Introduction

Growing up, I always dreamed that one day I would write the next "Great American Novel." To show how clever I was, I even told myself I would title it "The Next Great American Novel." Hey, I was fourteen at the time.

I am now well into middle age and I have yet to accomplish this goal. To date, I have not even written the next "Shockingly bad, suitable only for use as fireplace kindling in the event the power goes out" novel. I chalk this up to a short attention span and a long honey-do list.

What I have been able to accomplish, however, is the compilation of a series of short, amusing tales from my own life as a husband and father. The events described in these stories took place during the first fifteen years of my married life, when I was, arguably, a standard-issue adult male. Of course, that is not to say that I was completely mature or without fault. Fact-of-the-matter is, I remain, to this day, very much a work-in-progress.

In compiling these stories into a memoir, of sorts, I did not intend that it serve as a parenting or relationship "How to" guide. I understand that book stores already have plenty of them. Instead, I have accumulated a collection of short, humorous and, occasionally, moving anecdotes from my own experience as a husband and father in hopes that you, the reader, might find something relatable and, perhaps, even inspirational. If you leave with nothing more than a smile or a chuckle, that is perfectly fine. If you also learn something along the way, whether about yourself or the person snoring next to you, that's even better.

Each of the stories contained in this book is, to the best of my recollection, accurate and complete, warts and all. This, despite the directive from my lovely wife to write her thinner. Some of the stories have appeared previously in print and electronic magazines, others have never before seen the light of day. But all reflect the life and times of an average American male with a wife and two kids, struggling to maintain mastery over a domain that was never really under his control to begin with.

I hope you enjoy it. And if not, there's always the "How to" section of your local book store.

DO YOU COME HERE (TO WORK OUT) OFTEN?

So there I was at the gym, determined to reverse the first signs of a beer-belly, when an attractive, young brunette woman toting a small, transistor radio struck up a conversation. It went something like this:

"Is my radio bothering you?"

"No, not at all."

"If it is, I can dial it down a bit."

"No, its fine."

"Okay," she said, "but let me know if you change your mind."

"Actually, if you're willing to take requests, I wouldn't mind a little rock-and-roll."

"Not a fan of country music?" she asked.

"Well, it only brings up bad memories," I explained. "You see, my girl just left me for my best friend and my dog died when the guy repossessing my pickup truck ran it over."

This elicited an honest chuckle, and soon we were chatting like old friends. As our schedules seemed to coincide, over the next few weeks we became workout pals, sharing stories about our families, jobs and significant others in between improving our physiques. At the time, I had a serious girlfriend and, though unintentional, conversations with my workout pal frequently led me to be late for our dates.

When the girlfriend discovered that my workout pal was female, she was none too pleased. Despite my assurances that the relationship was plutonic, she insisted that I find someone else to converse with at the gym. Or better yet, change gyms altogether. Instead, I changed significant others, and just over a year later my workout pal became my wife.

How did I know that this slender girl with the transistor radio was the one? It wasn't the fact that she owned a pickup truck and drove it like Richard Petty. Or the fact that she had purchased her own house at the ripe old age of twenty-two.

No, the moment that comes to mind occurred during one of our very first dates. We were walking through a crowded art gallery following dinner at a trendy restaurant when she suddenly burped. Loud enough that it echoed against the walls of the previously silent room.

I looked about the gallery and immediately noticed a variety of pursed lips and furrowed brows on the faces of the snooty patrons.

Before I could process the situation further, my future bride turned and punched me in the arm.

"Disgusting!" she exclaimed with mock indignation.

"Sorry," came my sheepish reply.

And that was that. I was hopelessly smitten.

Not simply because this cute, little waif had belched in public, but also because she possessed the cojones to pass the blame on to me. What guy wouldn't appreciate such spunk?

So there you have it. From that moment on, I knew we were meant to be together. Just like I knew that somewhere out there, a country music artist was singing about losing his girl, his dog and his pickup truck.

A WORLD VIEWED THROUGH MAN EYES

I profess to being nothing if not a typical American male. In other words, I'm generally clueless when it comes to the female persuasion. I have tried to figure them out, but I've found it's easier understanding fluctuations in fuel prices.

So, it should have come as no surprise when, shortly after taking my marriage vows, I stumbled upon another significant difference between the sexes.

This discovery took place after my bride asked me to fetch the tweezers from a drawer in our bathroom. At the time, she was deployed across our bed, performing what appeared to be maintenance on her feet (like most men, I don't ask when it comes to a woman's feet), and I was strolling by on my way to the reading room.

Once in the bathroom, I searched the drawer from front to back but failed to locate the tweezers. So, I returned to the bedroom and offered her the nail clippers.

"These aren't the tweezers," she said.

"The tweezers aren't in the drawer. I thought these might work."

"The tweezers are in there," she replied.

I immediately took offense to her implication. "No they're not. I looked."

"Did you look with normal eyes?" she asked. "Or, did you use your *man eyes?*"

So there you have it. MAN EYES. I had never heard the term before, and it hit me square in the face, not unlike the first time I realized my parents weren't practicing celibacy.

Was there really such a thing as Man Eyes? How come I had never noticed the distinction before? Was I using them all of the time?

Of course, it was possible my wife was wrong. The theory required testing.

Before I could ponder the matter any further, my wife pulled me into the bathroom and opened the drawer. Then she moved aside a brush, a box of Q-tips and...there were the tweezers!

Like the cartoon character I sometimes appear to be, I performed a perfect double-take. In return, she offered me a sarcastic little smile.

"Obviously, you *were* using your man eyes," she declared. With that, she turned and marched triumphantly back into the bedroom.

So maybe there was some substance to the phenomenon, though it's funny that I don't ever remember the eye doctor saying: "Now read off the top row, but make sure you don't use your man eyes." And I wasn't altogether convinced my wife didn't carry the tweezers into the bathroom in the palm of her hand.

When I finished my reading break, I pressed her on the subject. She explained in her matter-of-fact way that men don't always think when they are looking for something – particularly if a woman initiates the search. We tend to place our brains on auto-pilot, which naturally leads to the deployment of man eyes. I suppose it might also account for our refusal to stop and ask directions.

Later that same week, I returned from a quick trip to the market with a half-gallon of natural vanilla ice cream. My favorite.

"Why didn't you buy French vanilla?" she asked – French vanilla being her favorite.

"This isn't French vanilla?" I replied, examining the package. "Darn, I must have been using my man eyes again."

THE SWEATSHIRT OFF MY BACK

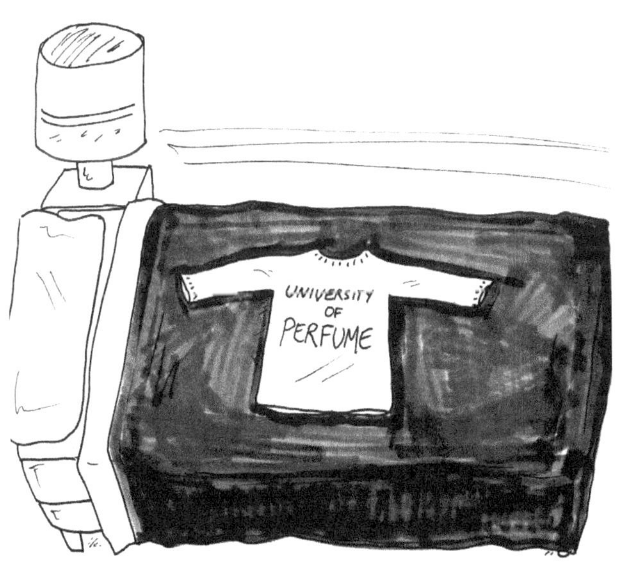

Sweatshirts are hotly contested turf in my house. I wouldn't say I'm obsessed with my sweatshirt collection – certainly no more so than I am with my hairline (pause to check for fallen follicles), but I do like them a lot.

My favorites are heavy and gray and emblazoned with the logos of my favorite college and sports teams. I also have fancier sweatshirts that work well as evening attire when matched with a fresh pair of jeans and clean, white sneakers. Then there are my yardwork sweatshirts, some rattier than others, each no longer qualified to remain in my standard rotation.

When you live in the Midwest, a good sweatshirt can be critical to a man's wardrobe. They are great for bumming around in during the winter, they work well with a pair of shorts on cool, spring days and, of course, they are mandatory attire on football weekends.

The problem is, my wife likes them too.

Shortly after we were married, I discovered one of her many golden rules with respect to clothes: "What's mine is mine, and what's yours is also mine."

Now, this is fine when it comes to borrowing a t-shirt from my endless supply, assuming ownership of a shirt that no longer fits me or wearing my coat when we are out on an unexpectedly cool evening. But when it comes to my sweatshirts – that's another thing altogether.

You see, she doesn't just wear them proudly, as I do. No, she has to stretch the cuffs out and roll them up, occasionally splitting them at the seam. Then, she yanks the bottom of the sweatshirt down so that it covers as much of her southern territory as possible. Finally, while wearing one of my pride-and-joys, she often chews absentmindedly on the collar, a seemingly-cute habit that leaves the collar frayed and, well, chewed on.

But worse than all these transgressions, when she's done with them they are returned smelling as if they were just used as mops in the Bath & Body Works store at the mall. And no amount of washing seems to completely eradicate that feminine odor.

Recently, I ordered a new sweatshirt from a catalogue circulated by my alma mater. Great colors, a cool version of the school logo, extra-thick cuffs – everything a sweatshirt maven could want. It arrived in the mail a few days before the weekend telecast of the big game, which I planned to watch at a buddy's football party.

The morning of the game, I threw it on and immediately recognized the pungent smell of soap mixed with perfume. EGADS!

"Honey?" I called out.

"Yes?" she answered, walking into the bedroom.

"Did you wear my new sweatshirt?"

"Oh, yeah. I threw it on yesterday before I ran to the market."

"But I'm getting together with the boys in an hour to watch the big game."

"So?"

"So it smells like...you."

"And that's a bad thing?"

"Not if you're a woman. But in case you haven't noticed…"

"Oh, big deal. You'll be the nicest smelling guy at the party, that's all."

"Right…Just what I was hoping for."

So, now you see what I have to deal with.

As for the football party, it didn't go all that badly. I even got hit on once or twice.

THEY SHOOT PONY CHAIRS, DON'T THEY?

It all started with a simple chair.

My wife and I had just purchased our first home together and faced the seemingly mundane task of decorating it. One Sunday afternoon, while wondering through the cavernous confines of a local furniture superstore, I spotted something that would soon have a profound effect upon my life: a small, curvy club chair covered in black-and-white pony fabric.

It was love at first sight.

Now the first thing to understand is, this event occurred during a period of time in which furniture dressed in pony and cow prints enjoyed a certain degree of popularity. I believe the style was classified as Southwest, though most people might know it by its more popular label – Mistake.

"We have to buy this chair," I said as I plopped down in it. "It's really cool."

"I don't think so," came my wife's reply.

"Why not?"

I really wanted to take it home.

"It's Southwest style, and I'm not doing our house that way."

She really did not.

"But its just one little chair," I said as if it were a lost puppy. "It needs a home."

"And a year from now, your puppy will be out of style," she replied. Then she turned and walked away.

"But it's already house-trained," I yelled after her.

Now the second thing to understand is, my wife graduated college as an interior design major and had been gainfully employed in her field for the preceding three years. So, this was a little like Joe Fan trying to tell Derek Jeter how to hit a baseball.

Still, I am nothing if not persistent, and I chipped away at her resolve like a woodpecker on a juicy piece of bark. A half-hour later, we drove away from the store with the cute, little puppy in the back of our SUV.

We proceeded to furnish our great room in an eclectic style that reasonably incorporated the pony chair. Much to my delight, the chair quickly became the subject of considerable conversation whenever our circle of friends came to visit. This, in turn, prompted me to take a much greater interest in our household decorating decisions – to my wife's complete and utter annoyance.

It seems the pony chair had opened my eyes to a whole new world in which I could assert my influence. A world of faux finishes and vibrant colors. Concrete countertops? What a cool idea!

Soon, I was freely opining on the color of our walls, the pattern of a new floor rug, even the selection of designer switchplate covers. Surprisingly, these things now mattered to me. After all, it was my home too.

Of course, my suggestions were usually rewarded with a "Who's the designer here, you or me?" retort, but I learned to let it pass. I knew that if I pestered her long enough, eventually I would wear her down and get my way.

I started watching HGTV and scanning the pages of Architectural Digest while riding a stationary bike at the gym. When I attended the local home remodeling show, I barely acknowledged the bikini girls splashing about at the hot tub display. During dinner parties, I extolled the virtues of Corian and the beauty of Stickley.

That is, until the night that disaster struck.

Home alone, I decided to install a lazy susan in a corner cabinet of our kitchen. While removing the existing cabinetry, I accidentally punctured the plumbing. By the time my wife returned, a number of our base cabinets were ruined.

This proved to be the last straw, and I was permanently forbidden from any involvement in future home decorating matters. While I could still leave my mark on our home's exterior, the interior was now off-limits. My designing skills were relegated to making intricate patterns in the lawn with our mower.

And the pony chair?

As predicted by my better half, the style quickly went the way of the dodo, and the chair was exiled to our basement, eventually suffering significant staining. One evening, I carried its worn hide to the curb with the rest of our trash. After setting it down, I stood for a moment and reflected on the creative impact it had made in my life.

Then, I gave it a good, hard kick and walked back inside.

Chapter Five

THE MALE BIOLOGICAL CLOCK

That ticking sound you might be hearing may actually be coming from a man.

It turns out that women are not the only sex on this planet to suffer from the physiological phenomenon known as a biological clock. Imbedded deep within their tough, frequently hairy and always smelly exteriors, men have a biological clock of their very own.

I know this because the alarm on mine began to blare the morning of my first wedding anniversary.

At the time, I was the ripe old age of thirty. Suddenly, visions of playing catch with my offspring began to flood my consciousness, visions in which I was forced to prop myself up with a cane or chase after them with a walker. These were soon followed by images of family wrestling matches ending prematurely when my back gave out, as well as neighborhood kids referring to me as gramps.

Of course, the solution was simple – I needed to get my lovely bride in a family way as soon as humanly possible. Unfortunately, a major hurdle stood between me and my dreams of propagation. You see, at the time my wife was a mere twenty-five years of age and still relatively new in her chosen profession. Convincing her to trade her youth for nine months of morning sickness, bloating and back pain was going to be about as easy as convincing a dog not to lick its own privates.

That evening, I decided to broach the subject between dinner and dessert at the local three-star restaurant.

After knocking on our wooden table for luck, I began: "So I was thinking of some ways we might save a little more money for that new car." This approach was designed to appeal to her inherent sense of frugality.

"Really? I'd love to hear them," she responded.

"Okay, well, one of the things I was thinking was, maybe you could go off the pill."

"I see…Then how would we keep from getting pregnant? The rhythm method won't work, since you don't have any."

"Ha-ha. Actually, I was thinking that, maybe, we could just take our chances. If it's meant to be, it's meant to be."

I tried to say this in a casual, laissez faire way. I probably would have pulled it off, too, if my voice hadn't cracked.

"This isn't about saving money, is it?" she asked. Even back then, she could read me like a comic book.

"I'm thirty!" I blurted out. "I'd like to have some hair left when our kids graduate high school."

Now, we had discussed our desires for children long before walking down the aisle, and our plan was to have our first child no later than my wife's thirtieth birthday. In her mind, that meant she had three-to-four more years to enjoy her pre-child-birth figure. In my mind, that plan suddenly made about as much sense as ordering an expensive dessert when the main course has completely satiated you.

A few minutes later, as we nibbled on our twelve dollar chocolate fountain, she proceeded to give me the best anniversary gift I could have imagined: "I think you're right," she suddenly announced. "We should think about having children a lot sooner."

"But what about our plan," I asked, looking that gift horse squarely in the mouth. "What about waiting until you are closer to thirty?"

"Well, I did want to do that. But you know what I want even more?"

"A husband who isn't fixated on his hairline?"

"No."

"A husband who is comfortable talking about his emotions?"

"Well, yes. But that's not it."

"A husband who understands women?"

"Now, you're just speaking gibberish."

"Fine," I said. "I give up."

"What I really want is to see you be a father to our children."

Fifteen months later, her wish came true with the birth of our first son.

As I write this, it's been more than ten years since that joyous occasion, and my back hasn't given out once.

Knock on wood.

GAME, SET, BIRTH

Both of my children were born during the summertime, when temperatures rise and tennis champions are crowned. As an avid follower of all things sports-related, I can tell you without hesitation that my oldest boy was born during the early rounds of the U.S. Open, while the younger one came along the day of the men's final at Wimbledon.

Of course, my lovely wife is not a fan of all my sports watching, particularly when it happens to take place while she is gripping a hospital bed and wearing out her Lamaze techniques in order to navigate those intensely-painful, ever-increasing contractions associated with natural childbirth. Unfortunately, the birthing rooms at our hospital were conveniently equipped with something more distracting than a multi-vehicle accident involving a truck load of agitated pigs: wall-mounted televisions.

After helping my wife get comfortable in the hospital's motorized bed during her labor with our first son, I sat down in a bedside chair and couldn't help but notice the television remote resting on a side table. It called to me in a soft, alluring whisper: "Pick me up, turn me on....Pick me up, turn me on....Pick me up, turn me on."

When the nurse arrived to check my wife's vital signs, I used the distraction to snatch up the remote and, casually, click on the television. Moments later, I was watching a high-level tennis match accompanied by grunts, groans and screams. I believe the tennis players may have also been making some noise.

My respite from reality was short-lived.

"What the heck do you think you're doing?" yelled the person who used to resemble my petite bride.

"I just thought--"

"You thought? You thought? How about thinking about all the suffering you're putting me through right now?"

"I didn't know you hated watching tennis so much."

Suddenly, she reached her hand out, grabbed hold of my shirt collar and yanked me right up out of the chair.

"I'm not talking about tennis, you @#$%&*!"

Like most men, I dislike seeing my significant other in pain, especially when that pain is causing them to speak in tongues, exhibit super-human strength and curse you with language that would make a plumber turn red.

Shortly thereafter, our nurse was subjected to a desperate, screaming plea for an epidural injection. Unfortunately, she turned me down.

From that point on, it was all a blur. In fact, I think I may have even briefly blacked out from the limited amount of oxygen that was reaching my brain as a result of my wife's death-grip on my collar.

But I'm not complaining. When it was all said and done, I was rewarded with a healthy baby boy. And I think my wife went easier on me than she did on her OBGYN when she saw him the next day. You see, he ended up missing her delivery when his tennis match went into overtime.

A SECRET CLUB FOR WOMEN ONLY

When I was growing up, I used to love watching reruns of the "Little Rascals" on television. One of my all-time favorite episodes was entitled "He-Man Woman Haters' Club." The Rascals form a boys-only club and hijinks and hilarity ensue.

While car shopping after the birth of our first child, I came to the realization that a certain segment of women in this country are card-carrying members of another exclusive club – a club espousing hatred for one of the most practical inventions of the Twentieth Century. I give you the "He-Woman Minivan Haters' Club."

I suspect that my wife is one of the founding members of this organization. When we first began dating, she drove a silver pickup with black stripes and an engine that rumbled and rattled and constantly threatened to break free of its mount and race off with the other wild horses. After meeting me for lunch, she would hop in the beast, wave sweetly, then lay down a patch of rubber exiting the parking lot that would make Jeff Gordon envious.

Once we married and had our first child, she grudgingly agreed to sell the pickup. I suggested we replace it with a minivan and suffered a severe case of tonguelash (the psychological cousin of whiplash).

What was I thinking, asking her to drive a "mom-mobile"?

After that, she drove only SUVs. And not just any SUVs, only those with the most horse power available – her automotive concession to motherhood.

During this period of time, she would host other new mothers for "play dates" with the kids. Occasionally, I would walk in on these get-togethers and discover what appeared to be a full-fledged meeting of the He-Woman Minivan Haters' Club. One of them would speak a secret language closely resembling baby talk, then the others would look at me and laugh. I swear I once even caught them performing some sort of secret handshake.

In most cases, I would immediately generate a lame excuse and exit the room, afraid one of them might suddenly announce the desire for a human sacrifice.

All this because of the minivan. I mean, have you seen the latest models? Sliding doors on both sides of the vehicle which move electronically. Seats that can be configured more ways than a Rubic's Cube. Television screens that drop down out of the ceiling like a gift from Heaven. If the auto makers ever produce a sound-proof glass wall between the front and rear seats, they might very well have created the perfect car.

Shortly after our second child came along, the lease on my wife's SUV came to an end. At the time, it had been a while since the last meeting of the Club and my wife had truly taken to motherhood. As a result, I thought I might broach the subject one more time.

"Honey," I said, "maybe we should finally look at leasing a minivan."

"Are you serious?"

A sign I should quit right then and there. But, like most men, it slipped past me like an anniversary date. Instead, I came back with: "Have you seen the latest models?"

Her forehead wrinkled, her eyes narrowed. "How many times do I have to say it before it sinks into your warped little brain? I am not now, nor ever, going to drive a mom-mobile!"

With that, she turned and walked into the nursery, slamming the door in my face.

The next week we leased another SUV. I still hold out hope that one day she will finally relent, and we will own a top-of-the-line minivan with all the bells and whistles.

Just don't ask me to drive it.

THE GRASS IS ALWAYS GREENER

When did the quality of one's lawn become such a suburban status symbol?

I used to live in a typical subdivision in a fairly typical Midwestern suburb. The homes were sturdy, two-story edifices, and the residents were conscientious about keeping them looking pristine.

Yet, it wasn't enough to simply apply a fresh coat of paint every few years. I quickly discovered that a lavish lawn was the ultimate goal. I even came to suspect that some of my fellow homeowners judged their neighbors character by the quality of the green between the street and their front doors.

Son: "Dad, can I go play at Tommy's house?"

Dad: "Are you kidding? Have you seen how bad their lawn looks?"

Son: "So?"

Dad: "So? So God only knows what goes on inside their home."

Son: "But Daaaad..."

Dad: "I said 'No'. Now go outside and help your sister fertilize."

The competition for best lawn in our sub was always quite fierce. My next-door-neighbor, ever the handyman, eventually installed a secondary pump to increase the amount of water dispersed by his sprinkler system. When it was in use, my shower pressure dropped so low I was forced to rinse my hair with my son's squirtgun.

Another guy on my block cut his lawn three or four times per week – whether it needed it or not. I even spotted him on his riding mower at night. And I thought the headlights on those things were merely for show.

As for me, well, the neighbors weren't sending their kids over to play at my house.

But I must explain. See, I was put at a distinct disadvantage because of our dog. A big, female dog. And let me tell you something about big, female dogs that you might not know: Their urine makes industrial acid seem as mild as apple juice.

Wherever she would squat, the grass immediately shriveled up and died. You could almost hear the poor, defenseless blades screaming in agony. Worse yet, nothing would grow back for what seemed like generations.

Once, I walked across the street to chat with the neighbor who, at the time, owned the best lawn on the block. Lets call him Mr. Green Jeans. Well, unbeknownst to me, the dog followed me over and began sniffing around Mr. Green Jean's lawn. I figured this out when he suddenly stopped breathing and I was forced to administer CPR.

Fortunately, our dog only liked to utilize a small portion of our property for her "business." Unfortunately, the spot she had selected was directly in front of the house, adjacent to the sidewalk.

The lawn in this location began to look so bad, even I could no longer ignore it. So I dug it up and replaced it with shrubs and woodchips.

It didn't take long for a number of the neighbors to compliment me on the "new landscaping." What they were really saying was: "It's about time you took care of that area. But we'll forgive your tardiness, if you promise not to let it happen again. Oh, and any time you want to have our kids over to play, let us know."

After that, I tried to get the dog to do her "business" in the woods behind our house. She wouldn't. When I encouraged her to do her business, she'd simply turn and look at me as if I were asking her to urinate in her living room.

Next, I attempted to hose down the affected areas of the lawn immediately after she finished her squat. But the exact locations were difficult to detect at eleven o'clock at night.

Eventually, I gave up.

My lawn became spotted once again. My character was whispered about at weekend barbecues. My kids were turned down for play dates. But, fortunately, the situation proved to be short-lived.

The following summer, we moved.

Chapter Nine

TABLE FOR DADDY

When our two boys were old enough to sit at a table without throwing their food, we began a tradition of eating out on Friday nights. This led us to sample every family-oriented eatery within driving distance. Most exciting were the times when we headed for a brand new establishment.

Of course, we weren't alone in our desire, and typically we would arrive to discover the restaurant lobby more crowded than the post office on April 15th. In such circumstances, I would drop the family off at the door, then embark on a mission to secure a prime parking space.

Now, at this point, I need to insert a bit of backstory: You see, I was raised by a mother who believed finding a good parking spot was one of the most important missions in life. On a par with cooking and religion, in fact.

At the mall, she would drive up and down the aisles, over and over again, frequently by-passing open spaces on the fringes of the lot, until a spot opened up near the entrance. And God save anyone who attempted to pull into a spot that she had seen first. Raised in such an environment, there was little chance I would develop rational parking habits.

On one particular Friday evening, I located a parking spot just the other side of the handicapped spaces, then ventured proudly inside to my waiting family.

"How long's the wait?" I asked, once I had located them among the throngs in the lobby.

"The hostess said thirty minutes," my wife replied. "So that means more like forty-five. If you want, we could go some place else."

"And give up the prime parking space I just snagged?" I said. "No way."

After breaking up a handful of fights between my less-than-angelic sons, failing to entertain them with my Sponge Bob impersonation and allowing them to use my arm for a game of hangman, I eventually heard the hostess broadcast the following message over the restaurant loudspeaker: "Table for Daddy. Table for Daddy."

"That's us!" my sons announced in unison. Followed immediately by "Personal jinx!"

"What's us?" I interjected.

"Table for Daddy."

"Table for Daddy?"

At this point, the mother of my children stepped in to let me know that the rugrats had volunteered to give our name to the hostess. "She asked them for a first name," explained my wife. "Apparently, to your sons, your first name is Daddy."

And that is the moment my personal identity officially changed from my given name to "Daddy."

Of course, I had already been a father for a number of years, and, with the possible exception of oozing diapers and projectile vomiting, I had never enjoyed anything more. But until that night at the restaurant, I had always sort of viewed myself as possessing a dual personality. There was the adult me: Breadwinner, husband, sports nut. And then there was Daddy: Human jungle gym, mock disciplinarian, pushover.

That night, for the first time, I realized there would never be a Me that wasn't also Daddy. The two personas had merged into one, and that one would enjoy the remainder of his life as the father of two sons.

And, of course, I wouldn't have it any other way.

A LESSON IN PHILOSOPHY

I am a firm believer in the wise, old adage, "What goes around, comes around." Some people may phrase it as, "You reap what you sow." Still others may advise, "You get what you deserve."

Each of these is a way of saying, in effect: If you do a good deed, you will benefit from the good deed of another. Maybe not today, maybe not tomorrow, but at some point during your life. Or, perhaps, once you arrive in the Great Hereafter – assuming that proves to be your final destination.

I also believe the converse is true. Thus, if you perform a bad deed, then...well, you get the idea.

I suppose you could liken this to the philosophy of karma. According to Buddhist teachings, karma is the force generated by a persons actions and determines the nature of that person's next existence. Create bad karma, you may appear in the next life as an earthworm in a bait container.

Now, some people may dismiss these sorts of events as mere coincidence, and it's certainly difficult to prove them wrong. But even if they are correct, the world would undoubtedly be a better place if everyone went about their business as if the principle of karma were the law.

Over the years, I have tried to instill a little of this philosophy in my sons, but it has proven to be a difficult concept to grasp for a generation that has grown accustomed to instant gratification.

Still, I have to try.

Thus, when my younger son came to me complaining that his older brother was picking on him, I took the development as an opportunity to enlighten him.

"Have I ever told you about something called, 'What goes around, comes around?'" I asked.

He gave me a look that said, "Oh, no, not another one of Dad's goofy lessons. Why did I open my mouth?"

Unfazed by his rolling eyes, I continued: "What this means is, if you do something bad to someone, eventually something bad is going to happen to you. It's a thing some people call karma."

"Isn't that one of those new cars down at the auto show?" he asked.

"No, it's a philosophy that certain people believe in and live their lives by."

"Philoso—what?"

"Okay, look at it like this: Your brother picks on you, which is a bad thing. Right?"

Vigorous nodding.

"Well, someday someone bigger is going to pick on him, and he'll learn what it feels like. Then, maybe he'll think twice before he picks on you."

"Cool. When is that gonna happen?"

"I don't know. It may not happen for a while, but it will happen. That's what it means when I say, 'What goes around, comes around.'"

He pondered this lesson for a moment, then said, "Can't you just take away his Xbox?"

So, maybe he was a bit too young for a lesson in philoso-what, but someday he will understand the principle I was trying to impart.

After all, practical examples of karma occur all around us. I recall the road-rage story that appeared in the media a few years back. Apparently, one impatient fellow was tailgating a slower driver, causing the one in front to tap his brakes to warn the guy in back that he was getting too close. This only served to enrage the tailgater even more. He eventually pulled around the lead car and screeched to a halt – forcing the slower driver to stop. Then, blind with rage, the tailgater jumped out of his car and proceeded to kick and punch the other fellow's car as a stream of expletives spewed from his mouth like bubbles from a bubble wand. While all of this was going on, another motorist drove by and accidentally struck the tailgater, killing him.

Now one might surmise from these events that the tailgater was not a believer in the adage, "What goes around, comes around."

But something tells me he will change his mind when, in the next life, he looks in the mirror and sees and earthworm staring back.

ROUGHING IT

One summer I arranged a leisure-time activity that would prove to have a profound and lasting impact upon our family unit. This mind-blowing experience?

Camping.

Now bear in mind, I grew up in a family that simply did not camp, and I have always envied my friends and their captivating tales of communing with nature, sharing stories around a crackling campfire and sleeping under the stars. With two young boys of my own, I decided that I owed them the experience I had missed out on as a youth.

Of course, convincing my wife to go along with this plan was far from easy. Her definition of roughing it included staying in a hotel with less than three stars and continental rather than full breakfast. Consequently, I was quite surprised when I obtained her acquiescence with the mere offer of a future vacation in Hawaii, sans children.

Two weeks later, we were off to a well-known state park with camping equipment borrowed from our outdoorsy neighbors. The first sign of trouble occurred two hours into the three-hour drive, when I realized we had forgotten to pack my special-order, hypo-allergenic, orthopedic-support pillow. Ignoring my first thought – feigning illness and turning the vehicle around – I mustered up the courage to be a trooper and go three nights without it. After all, this trip wasn't for me, it was for my boys.

Shortly thereafter, we arrived at our campsite and unloaded our SUV. This led to a two-hour battle with an evil entity commonly referred to as a tent. Having no instruction manual and little personal aptitude, I found the pile of vinyl sheets, nylon ropes and aluminum poles more perplexing than a Chinese crossword puzzle. Eventually, I was able to utilize the learning acquired from two advanced degrees to produce something that resembled a lopsided teepee.

"Dad, are you sure that's how its supposed to look?" asked my curious younger son.

"Yes," I lied.

"Woo-woo, woo-woo…Woo-woo, woo-woo…" sang my sarcastic older son while tapping his mouth and performing an improvised rain dance around our teepee.

While my wife attempted to squeeze a week's worth of gear into our home-away-from-home, I moved on to starting our first campfire. This proved to be a much less daunting task, thanks to a half-a-can of lighter fluid.

With dinner out of the way and marshmallows roasting on sticks, I figured the time was right to tell my first campfire scary story. Yet, when I finished my tale of headless zombies roaming through the darkened woods in search of fresh meat, I was met, not with applause, but with the cries of two petrified little boys who refused to spend the night in a flimsy teepee-tent.

Later, while attempting to coax them into their sleeping bags, I noticed a phenomenon I had not previously considered: The interior of our tent was as hot and humid as the air on the outside. Accustomed to sleeping in a climate-controlled seventy degrees, I immediately began to fret.

And sweat.

"Just lay on top of the sleeping bag," my wife suggested in her matter-of-fact way.

"Good idea," I responded.

Yet, not only did this fail to cool me off, it provided the handful of mosquitoes buzzing about the interior of our porous abode with a feast fit for a king. I swear I heard one of the little fellow's exclaim, "The buffet's open!"

Perspiration seeping from my pores like oil from a jalopy, bug-bites rising across my extremities like lumps on the back of a toad, I finally gave up and headed for our SUV. That night, my boys and I slept in the vehicle with the motor running and the air conditioning blowing. Meanwhile, my high-maintenance wife was the only one who actually roughed it.

When morning came, we admitted defeat, packed up our gear and headed home. Since then, my boys have developed an unnatural fear of marshmallows, and I have endured a recurring nightmare involving teepees filled with headless zombies.

My wife? She has taken to sleeping in the backyard beneath the stars. She says she's even thinking about booking us a grass hut when I take her to Hawaii.

I just hope it comes with zombie repellant.

OH MOE, WHERE ART THOU?

If you are anything like me – knee-deep in middle age and not entirely happy about it – then you probably grew up watching the classics on television.

Of course, by classics I'm referring to The Little Rascals, Three Stooges and Abbott and Costello.

These shows were an after-school staple in my neighborhood. If the day proved to be cold or rainy, we would park it in front of the nineteen-inch and laugh out-loud at the antics of Moe, Larry and Curly, or Spanky, Alfalfa and the beautiful Darla (Miley Cyrus, eat your heart out).

Now you have to remember, this was in the days before basic cable, or the Dark Ages as my children like to refer to them. In fact, there was only one channel broadcasting children's programming during weekday afternoons, though occasionally we could pick up a Canadian station if Venus and Mars were aligned just right.

Still, it didn't matter one poke-in-the-eye that we'd seen each episode ten times before. These shows featured real people performing real stunts and making us emit real laughter.

Thinking about Moe using the width of his hand to block Larry's two-fingered eye-poke still makes me chuckle today. Or, a bald-headed Curly slapping himself repeatedly across the face before scattering a group of bad guys like bowling pins.

Things are different today. Children's programming is mostly animated, and there is a plethora of options for every age group. You've got a circle of talking babies (Rugrats), a bumbling boy genius (Jimmy Neutron) and a comic sea sponge (SpongeBob).

Now, don't get me wrong, I am not completely opposed to today's programming for children. I've actually laughed while watching the Sponge and his starfish buddy, and many Rugrat episodes seem to contain a positive message. But I also lament the fact that my kids aren't exposed to some of the classic shows of my youth.

So one summer I rented a few dvds containing episodes of The Little Rascals and Three Stooges prior to taking the family on a driving vacation. Thanks to our vehicle's built-in entertainment center, my children were going to enjoy some good, old-fashioned guffaws on our trip.

"Believe me, you guys are gonna love this stuff," I promised them.

"Dad?"

"Yeah?"

"What's a stooge?"

The answer to this age-old question would become apparent shortly after we hit the road.

With my wife behind the wheel, I climbed in the back to watch one of the dvds with my kids. Now they'd witness physical comedy at its finest.

Yet, to my complete and utter surprise, for the next hour my children sat stone-faced, with nary a "nyuk, nyuk" slipping from their lips. In fact, they actually took offense to some of the slapstick.

"Why does Moe always poke Larry in the eyes?" asked my youngest.

"Because it's funny," I explained.

"It doesn't look like Larry thinks it's funny."

"Yeah," my eldest chimed in, "and why is Curly named Curly? I mean, the dude's got less hair on his head than you do."

Unfazed, I popped out the disc and replaced it with The Little Rascals. Unfortunately, my children failed to relate in any meaningful way to Spanky and the gang. This became all too apparent when one of them asked me why Buckwheat doesn't comb his hair.

Ultimately, my grand experiment proved to be a complete dud. Perhaps it was the lack of color or the naked realism that put my kids off; I don't really know for sure. What I can say is, barely an hour after firing up the first dvd, my children asked me to turn it off so they could stare out the window.

I guess I should chalk it up to the fact that my kids and I are the products of significantly different eras. What is funny to one generation may not prove humorous to another. Then again, I might be missing the boat altogether.

The one thing I'm sure of? From now on I'll be keeping my nyuks to myself.

BACK TO SCHOOL

Like millions of parents around the country, the end of every summer prompts my wife and I celebrate the national holiday known as Kids Go Back to School Day!

This event generally begins with a trip to the local elementary school to pick up a list of required supplies for the coming year. Of course, with each passing year the list grows larger.

Two different types of writing instruments. Three different types of glue. Are we preparing our children for school, or stocking our educators' supply closet?

Back when I was a kid, we got by with one type of glue – Elmers. It was supplied by our teacher, who warned us that eating it would cause our intestines to stick together, leading to a painful blockage and, eventually, an explosion that would scatter feces up to a mile away.

Of course, this only served to increase our desire to dine on the sticky white substance. And no one, to my knowledge, ever suffered a gastric catastrophe – at least, not from ingesting Elmers.

Also appearing on my children's list: a Dictionary and Thesaurus.

What a second-grader needs with a Thesaurus, I'm not sure I really know. I suppose he could use it to identify new ways to call his brother a doofus when they pass each other in the school hallway, but beyond that I'm at a loss.

Then there are the sticky notes, to be supplied in at least four different colors.

It seems to me that one color is sufficient, since most of them will likely end up stuck to the back of some unsuspecting student emblazoned with the words "kick me."

Scanning a recent school supply list, one with more line items than my oldest's Christmas list the year I told him to knock himself out, my eyes fixated upon a single entry: financial calculator.

This led to an obvious question: Who was supposed to be doing the work, my son or Texas Instruments?

Finding little explanation on the supply list, I did what any self-respecting parent would do: I loaded the wife and kids into the family SUV and motored to the nearest Walmart.

Walking in the entrance, we were immediately greeted by a giant tube of toothpaste. Wielding an oversized toothbrush like a light saber, the green-and-white cylinder sang and danced and caused a few small children to run screaming to their mommies. One can only imagine the damage that will eventually be inflicted upon them by an unnatural fear of dental hygiene.

Avoiding the toothpaste as if it was a door-to-door salesman, we made for an aisle that teemed with pre-pubescence – the aisle marked "Back to School."

As my boys pushed their way to the shelves, I stumbled upon a table marked 75% Off. Among the items scattered about the table were various styles of three-ring-binder.

A light-bulb flipped on: These were on the list!

"Hey, guys, look at what I found," I called out, holding up a pair of binders. "Pretty neat, huh?"

"Daaaad, those are Pokemon binders," noted my youngest.

"I know," I said with a smile.

"Those are so last year," opined my oldest.

"Yeah, not cool," added my youngest, sending the remnants of my smile to the recycle bin.

Then my wife held up a pair of Sponge Bob notebooks.

"Alright Mom!" and "Awesome!" came the youthful responses.

"And how about these soccer ball erasers?" she asked.

"Sweet!"

"Cool!"

Seeing that I was about as useful as a Pokemon lunchbox, I retreated to a corner. Glancing about, I noticed a shelf lined with a large variety of glues, including good, old Elmers.

That's when I discovered that, while some things change with the passage of time, other things stay very much the same.

Like the taste of a certain glue, for instance.

SPARE THE BELT, SPOIL THE CHILD?

Most people over the age of thirty have vivid memories of some form of corporeal punishment inflicted upon them by their parents during childhood. In my house, the instrument of choice was the belt. But it was also much more than that.

If my brother or I stepped seriously out of line, we were ordered to march immediately to our parents' closet and retrieve a belt. Once the belt had been delivered, we were made to bend over and succumb to an appropriate number of lashes, depending upon the severity of our infraction.

We were never struck hard enough to inflict injury. In reality, the worst part of this punishment was "The Walk" – the journey to and from the closet. It amounted to a mild form of psychological torture, something akin to the time I informed my younger brother he was adopted after replacing his birth certificate with homemade adoption papers.

After considerable practice brought on by numerous infractions, I developed the "medium slow" walk, meaning slow enough to buy some time in hopes that an interruption (the phone, the doorbell, the dog soiling the carpet) might delay and, therefore, lessen the impact of the inevitable, but not so slow as to increase the offended parent's wrath.

I can remember a neighbor stopping by while I was on The Walk, then staying for more than an hour. Afterward, my mother decided to forgo the belt entirely, grounding me for the weekend instead. I felt so indebted to the neighbor, I vowed never again to toilet paper her house on Devil's Night.

Of course, I tried other tricks to lessen the severity of the belt, especially if the parent giving the marching order was my heavy-handed father. The most famous of these was the retrieval of the terry-cloth belt from his bathrobe. He laughed so hard he eventually granted me a one-time pass.

Shortly after meeting my bride-to-be, we compared notes regarding our respective childhood's. When I told her about The Walk, she laughed.

Turns out, she was forced to retrieve a red slipper from her parents' closet when she incurred their wrath. The red slipper had a hard rubber sole, so it quickly became a feared form of punishment in her house.

Like most people I know, my wife and I turned out okay in spite of (or, possibly, because of) the corporeal punishment we endured as children. Yet, when we had children of our own, we immediately decided we would forgo physical punishment, instead employing timeouts and the denial of privileges to deter undesirable behavior. This seemed to be consistent with the preferred methods of discipline in modern society.

As time went by, however, I began to wonder how effective it truly was. Then, I had an opportunity to revisit the "old ways" when I caught my younger son in a series of lies.

"Go to Mom and Dad's closet and get me a belt," I ordered in a gruff voice.

"Why?" came his timid response.

"Because it's time for a good, old-fashioned spanking."

He looked at me like my head had just separated from my body and begun spinning like a top.

"Now go!"

Slowly, he began The Walk. Confused and scared, I'm sure he longed for the days when his punishment was tied directly to the amount of time he got to play video games.

Meanwhile, I started to feel really bad – who was being punished again? I quickly decided corporeal punishment was one parenting method that was best left in the history banks.

A few moments later, my son came trudging back like a prisoner headed for the guillotine.

As he approached, I was about to inform him that I had changed my mind when I saw it dangling from his right hand, recognizable by its texture and width:

The belt from my bathrobe.

CALL ME MR. FIX-IT

I needed a new lawnmower.

This, of course, is only significant if your lawn is beginning to resemble the grassy plains of the Serengeti.

As it so happened, I had ventured into the backyard and nearly confused our golden retriever for a prowling lion. After taking a second glance to confirm the shaggy creature was indeed canine, I maneuvered past a group of grazing gazelles and headed for the garage.

Pulling out our ten-year-old Craftsman mower, I berated the mute machine for quitting on me a month before.

"After all we've been through," I said with more than a hint of indignation.

Actually, the engine still ran, but the self-propelled mechanics had suddenly stopped propelling, turning the formerly easy to push cutting machine into a block of heavy metal that would barely budge if given a set of skis and shoved out of the starting gate at the Olympic ski jump.

And, of course, I vowed to run naked through my town before I dragged the immobile beast across our large, undulating yard.

Still, with the cutting season nearly over, the prospect of sinking a wad of cash into a new mower thrilled me about as much as a jury-duty notice.

"Whatcha doing, Dad?"

My younger son had joined me in the garage.

"I'm about to take the old mower apart to see if I can fix it."

"No, really, what are you doing?"

"What's that supposed to mean? You don't think your old man can fix things?"

He didn't even hesitate.

"Remember when you tried to put my new bike together?"

"Yeah...So?"

"You turned it into a unicycle!"

"That's because it was defective," I lied.

"Actually, that's the same word used by the man at the bike store when Mom had him fix it. Except I don't think he was talking about the bike."

"Speaking of Mom, isn't she calling your name right now?"

"I don't hear anything," he responded.

"Yep. You'd better go see what she wants."

After I had gotten rid of him, I unscrewed the plastic cover that protected the self-propelling apparatus, then stared hard at the gears, belts and suspenders. Everything appeared to be in working order.

I started the engine, shifted the thing into drive.

A little arm seemed to release, a belt began to turn, then so did the gears. Still, the wheels held firm. Like the derrieres of my children when seated in front of a video game.

I turned it off, then pulled on this and pushed on that. Satisfied with my efforts, I started the mower once again but, alas, no improvement.

A half-hour later, I had a badly scraped knuckle, a cut on my thumb and a sore foot – courtesy of a well-placed kick – but the lawnmower wasn't budging.

Fortunately, my other foot was spared by my wife's call for lunch.

With my batteries recharged from soup and a sandwich, I returned to the garage and, by day's end, my over-grown lawn was completely neat and trim.

Shortly thereafter, the residents of my little town may or may not have been treated to the sight of a naked man jogging along the sidewalk with his bandaged hands covering his privates.

THE MAGIC OF CHRISTMAS

Ah, the holidays...Pushy shoppers, inflated prices, short tempers – and that's during the bake sale at my kids' elementary school.

Sometimes I wonder why I look forward to this time of year with such exuberance. But then my children will do something selfless and unexpected and, like Aunt Betty's fruitcake, my doubts are shelved until the next holiday season.

Take Christmas a few years back, for instance. A couple weeks before the big day, my six-year-old decided that he needed to personally deliver his Christmas list to Santa. So, we journeyed to the one place where you are certain to find the Jolly Old Elf in person – the local mall.

Of course, my oldest complained the entire way. It seems that at some point during the preceding year, he had made the conversion to non-believer. I had approached him on the subject the day before. Our discussion went something like this:

Me: "So, you don't believe in Santa?"

Him: "Nope."

Me: "How you can be so sure?"

Him: "I don't know. I just am."

Me: "Well, what if you're wrong? You know he only brings presents to those who believe in him."

Him: "Come on, Dad, everyone knows Santa Claus is just

a myth created by the toy companies so they can reduce year-end inventory."

Me: "Yeah, well, you better watch out, or you might just find a lump of coal in your stocking."

Him: "Oooh, I'm really scared!"

With my eldest a lost cause, I focused on preserving the magic of Christmas for my younger son. My determination was immediately tested on the drive to the mall.

"Explain to me again how there can be so many Santas running around?" asked my eldest.

"Those are his helpers," I snorted. Then my wife threw him a nasty look for good measure.

"Yeah," added my youngest. "Each one is an elf."

"Oh, right," said the Grinch seated next to him. "Then it would probably hurt if I pulled on his beard."

I eyed him in the rearview mirror. "You can bet it's gonna hurt!"

The threat seemed to register, and soon my two boys immersed themselves in a line-by-line comparison of their Christmas lists. Wouldn't want there to be any duplicates...

Moments later we were inside the mall and maneuvering through hordes of glassy-eyed shoppers. That's when I spotted it: A line of people extending as far as the eye could see.

The line to visit Santa Claus.

Now, I'm not saying the line was long, but I did notice some of the parents had brought along tutors for their children.

Of course, my first reaction was to make a u-turn and leave.

Then, I noticed the look in my younger son's eyes, and I knew I wasn't going anywhere.

After a wait that seemed to last longer than the movie "Gigli," we finally approached the head of the line. I glanced over to the jolly figure seated on the throne and, darn, if he didn't look like the real McClaus, er, McCoy. If I hadn't known any better, I'd swear...

At this point, a female elf walked up to escort my oldest son. I looked down, and he was nothing but grins and goose bumps. As he climbed onto Santa's lap, he actually looked three again. I watched as he whispered in the Merry One's ear, and they shared a few chuckles.

When he came back to us, there was a sparkle in his eye and spring in his step. I almost wanted to send a search party to look for my real son.

Next, my youngest took center stage. I moved a little closer and heard Santa ask him: "What's the one thing you want most this Christmas?"

He didn't hesitate. "I want my brother to believe in you," he said in his little boy voice.

Santa smiled. "Oh, he does, little one. He does."

Then the Jolly Old Elf gave me a wink, and I began to think that just about anything was possible.

Except, of course, eating Aunt Betty's fruitcake.

HERE COME THE SOCCER DADS

When I was growing up, I was among the tiny minority of children who played the sport of soccer. To most of my friends, soccer was nothing more than a goofy activity you participated in during gym class, usually sandwiched between flag football and floor hockey. "Goofy," because it relied upon foot-eye coordination, a skill only a handful of outcasts and an exchange-student named Manuel seemed to possess.

Things are much different today. More children play youth soccer than any other sport in America. There are teams for every level of play, from flower-picker to superstar. I know this because my oldest son has played soccer since the age of four, and he is now a highly-skilled member of a "travel" team.

And as his proud father, I have been exposed to a unique but growing fraternity of men known as the Soccer Dads.

What does it mean to be a member of this fraternity?

First of all, a Soccer Dad is someone who did not play competitive soccer at any level while growing up. Soccer Dad played baseball, football, maybe basketball, but he considered the sport of soccer something only foreigners were serious about.

Now that his kids play the sport, Soccer Dad will run around with them in the yard, kicking the ball here and there and looking somewhat mystified when his kids dribble it through his legs.

Soccer Dad may also form an adult team with other Soccer Dads, thereby transforming the sport into something that looks suspiciously like rugby. Only with a lot more pulled groins and stubbed toes.

Watching his kids' games, however, is where Soccer Dad really makes his mark.

First of all, he clearly has confused attending a soccer match with a football game. I say this because Soccer Dad will yell as if he is at a football stadium filled with a crowd of 50,000 rabid fans. Only he is at the local park with a dozen parents watching two teams of eight-year-old girls scamper about.

Soccer Dad yells things like: "Hey, ref, that was a good, clean hit!"

Or: "Don't let her push you around, Pumpkin!"

Followed by: "Offsides? Offsides? But the ball was never snapped!"

Worse yet, Soccer Dad will often volunteer to coach his child's team. Although he should be admired for his willingness to get involved, his lack of knowledge will often result in a team that is best known for its delicious post-game snacks.

Still, I don't want to sound too critical of Soccer Dad. On a positive note, his enthusiasm can, at times, be catching. He truly cares about what happens during the games, even if he doesn't always understand it.

Soccer Dads are also at least partly responsible for one particular phenomenon that should be adapted to many other sports: The post-game tunnel. This is where parents face each other in a line, clasp hands and form a human tunnel through which the players – win or lose – run while their parents yell something unintelligible. Even a miserable defeat can be salved with a jaunt through the parent tunnel.

So, in retrospect, I guess there is a place for Soccer Dads in my soccer world.

Especially if they continue to provide those great post-game snacks.

A TRIP DOWN MEMORY LANE

They grow up fast, don't they?

Shortly before my oldest son celebrated his tenth birthday, I drove him to a local college campus to attend his first overnight sports camp.

Of course, Baby Elvis, as we nicknamed him at birth upon seeing his thick, dark hair and long sideburns, had already been religiously watching ESPN's "Sports Center" for the better part of a year.

The sports camp was a five-day, four-night training program for advanced-level soccer players and included room and board in an authentic, begging-to-be-condemned freshman dormitory.

As we lugged his bags down the narrow hallway to room 128, I experienced a flashback to my first days as a freshman, many moons before.

When I had left my suburban home for college, disco had just died and new wave music was actually "new." Yet some things can still trigger a vivid memory of those halcyon days; things like the pungent, musty odor I detected the moment I walked into room 128.

"Wow. I'd forgotten what these rooms smell like."

"You didn't go to school here, Dad."

"No, but believe me – dorm rooms all smell the same."

"You mean, like some old guy's jockstrap?"

"You'll get used to it. In fact, once the year is up, you'll actually find you miss the smell."

"Yeah, except I'm only gonna be here for five days."

"Oh, right. Well, maybe you won't get used to it."

I busied myself by helping unpack the month's worth of clothes, sundries and snacks his mother had packed for him. The kid had more pairs of button-fly undershorts than Joe Boxer. He could have changed hourly and still returned home with a handful of clean ones.

"Mom went a little crazy, eh?" I remarked.

"Dad, you packed my clothes."

"Hey, better safe than sorry."

Soon, music was blaring from his boom box and kids were strolling in to say "Yo" and munch on his snacks.

I sat in the corner and tried to make sense of the memories and emotions racing through my mind.

"You okay, Dad?" he asked, noticing my silence.

"What? Oh, yeah, I'm fine. I was just thinking about the past. And the future."

"You mean like when I go to college?"

"Yeah."

"What was your first day of college like?"

"You really want to know?"

"Yeah."

I considered telling him about how my anxiety had led me to go to a party with some kids I had just met and, wanting desperately to fit in, to drink way too much alcohol.

Before I could respond, a staff member stuck his head in the room to fetch the boys for their orientation meeting.

I gave my son a hug goodbye and headed for the car.

The next evening I returned, partly to bring him the alarm clock he'd forgotten, partly to see how he'd done that first night.

As it turned out, he'd woken up around two a.m. with a bout of nausea that eventually led to an hour of clutching the toilet and vomiting. Mild food poisoning was the diagnosis.

"I've been okay all day today," he insisted in response to my concerned expression.

"You sure?"

"Yeah. Stop worrying."

We sat together for a moment without saying a word.

"Hey," I finally said, wrapping my arm around his boney shoulders, "remember when you asked me what my first day of college was like?"

"Yeah?"

"Well, now you know."

Chapter Nineteen

THE ONLY WAY TO FLY

If you've never flown first class, I've got three words of advice for you: Don't do it! The experience will ruin you, making it impossible to ever fly coach again.

Recently, I took the family to California for some much needed rest and relaxation. Due to the length of the flight and an unusual amount of frequent-flyer miles, I decided to go all-out and bump all four of our coach tickets up to first class. Neither I nor my wife had flown first class before.

We were first-class virgins.

The benefits of our status began moments after entering the terminal. We stepped to the end of a lengthy line at the security checkpoint, and an imposing security official scanned our tickets.

"Oh, you're first-class passengers," he noted with a smile. "Please follow me."

We did as we were told, and he led us to a separate checkpoint for those traveling in first class. Friendly faces greeted us and helping hands loaded our bags onto the x-ray conveyor. Best of all – no waiting! When they handed me back my leather shoes, I swear they even looked newly polished.

At our departure gate, we ran into the parents of a classmate of our oldest son. It turned out they were taking the same flight to California.

As we stood talking, a female voice announced, "We are now pre-boarding all passengers sitting in first class and first class only. Those of you among the coach herd, please wait in the pen to the left of the gate."

We grabbed our carry-ons and began moving toward the gate as the other couple eyed us suspiciously.

"We used our frequent-flyer miles to move up to first class," explained my embarrassed wife.

"I see," snorted the other wife.

"Yeah, we've never done this before," I added.

"Ooh la la," replied the other husband, his voice dripping with sarcasm.

Once we entered the cabin, a bevy of stewardesses immediately surrounded us, taking our coats to the first-class coat closet, storing our carry-ons in the overhead compartment, helping us get comfortable in the extra-wide seats. I think I even heard one of them offer us a pre-flight massage.

As my boys began playing with every button and doodad in sight, a stewardess named Heidi appeared.

"I will be taking care of you during today's flight," she said with complete earnestness. "Would either of you care for a drink?"

Across the aisle, I heard a distinguished gentleman order a glass of Chardonnay.

"Yes. A couple Chardonnays, please," I replied, figuring we could afford to have at least one adult beverage.

As Heidi filled my glass, I pulled out some cash.

"Oh, Sir – the beverages are complimentary in first class," she said.

"Right…I knew that."

My frugal wife then quickly chimed in, "Please leave the bottle."

By the time we were an hour into our flight, we had finished off the bottle and were feeling no pain. In fact, when my children returned from the lavatory playing catch with a roll of toilet paper, I remarked, "How cute."

A short while later, Heidi re-appeared to take our dinner orders.

"Tonight you have two choices," she informed us. "Lemongrass-steamed Icelandic salmon reposed on a bed of garlic mashed potatoes and surrounded by sauteed green beans. Or beef tenderloin with duxelles of Portobelo mushroom and potato scallops wrapped in filo dough and baked en terrine."

After wiping the drool off my chin, I composed myself long enough to order the salmon. Then I asked Heidi an important question.

"Just out of curiosity, what are the meal choices for passengers in coach?"

"I believe they have a choice of either Italian or turkey sub," she replied.

"Ooh la la," I said to my wife, and the two of us shared a conspiratorial smile.

Once I had topped the meal off with a healthy slice of raspberry cheesecake, I loosened my belt and took a satisfying sip from my little glass of Baileys.

My equally-satiated wife turned toward me, a frown upon her face.

"What's wrong?" I asked.

"I was just thinking," she said. "I'm never gonna be able to fly coach again."

"Oh, come on–"

"I'm serious," she replied. "This flight has totally ruined me."

"Well, let's not worry about tomorrow," I suggested. "Let's just enjoy today."

With that, I took a bite from one of the chocolate-dipped strawberries Heidi had just deposited on each of our trays and closed my eyes.

Unfortunately, the five-hour flight proved way too short, and soon we were crowded around the luggage carrousel with the peons from coach.

Before we could grab our bags and escape, our friends from home stopped us.

"So, how were the accommodations in first class?" snarled the husband.

"Ooh la la," I replied.

And I meant every word.

JURY DUTY

When my wife received a jury duty questionnaire in the mail, she immediately asked me for help with filling it out.

Of course, she wasn't seeking my legal expertise in order to complete the questionnaire more accurately. No, my saintly wife was hoping I could assist her in achieving her rejection from the juror pool.

Now many people (including yours truly) believe that it is our civic duty to serve on a jury when called. We have no standing to complain about "the system" if we aren't willing to participate in it.

There are many other people, however, who view jury duty as nothing more than a major pain in the hind quarters and go to great lengths to obtain pain relief.

Apparently, my wife falls into the latter category.

Not one to run from a woman in need of assistance – particularly if I happen to share my bed with said woman – I agreed to look over the questionnaire and offer her some advice.

After doing so, I came up with the following proposed answers to some of the questions:

Q: Are you a citizen of the United States?

A: I don't know, does crossing the border in the trunk of a car during the middle of the night make me a citizen?

Q: Have you ever been a law enforcement officer?

A: No, but I have made plenty of citizen arrests. Does that count?

Q: Have you served as a juror during the past 12 months?

A: No. Usually I move to a new state when I receive this notice in the mail.

Q: Do you have a permanent physical or mental disability that would interfere with or prevent you from serving as a juror?

A: Permanent? No, it's only a temporary condition that strikes whenever I sit for any length of time with a group of my peers.

Q: Have you ever been involved in a criminal lawsuit?

A: Yes, but it was against my will.

Q: Have you ever been convicted of a felony?

A: Convicted? Not really.

Q: Have you ever been confined in any correctional facility or prison?

A: No, I've always been able to escape.

Q: Are you presently employed?

A: Yes, at the local branch of the U.S. Post Office. But I've been under a lot of stress lately, and I've just about had all that I can take.

Q: List any other occupations you have held during the last 10 years?

A: Counterfeiter, safecracker, cat burglar, extortionist, jaywalker.

When I turned these model answers over to my wife, she failed to see the humor in them. She did, however, find plenty of humor in the way I hopped about on one leg after she kicked me in the shin.

WHEN IT COMES TO SPOONING, I'M A FORK

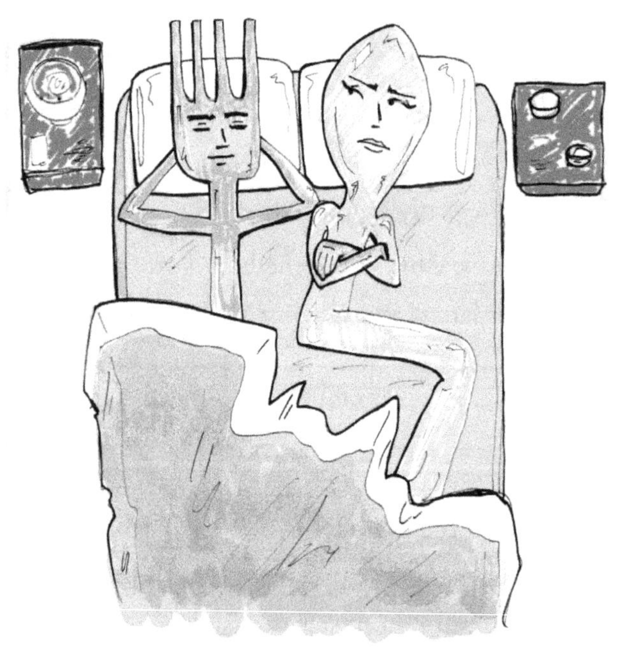

I may be a full-fledged, red-blooded consumer, but when my wife attempted to sell me on the idea that a man invented spooning, well, I just wasn't buying it.

Of course, this conversation sprung from her continual efforts to convince me to spoon with her while we slept, and my continual efforts to avoid the position by pretending I was a fork.

Now, I believe I am as romantic as the next guy (especially if that guy happens to be a sports-addicted, anniversary-date-forgetting everyman), but when I go to sleep I typically need a little space. And space is the antithesis of what you get when engaged in the act of spooning. Not to mention the fact that when I'm forced to sleep on my side, I usually wake up in the middle of the night screaming: "They've amputated my arm! They've amputated my arm!"

No, for most men, spooning is sort of like being pregnant – sure, we understand how it works but, physically, we simply can't do it.

The issue of spooning really touches on a somewhat larger subject: The conflicting sleeping habits of men and women.

Take my house, for instance. I cannot fall asleep unless it's at or below seventy degrees in our bedroom. Just can't do it. I will toss and turn, flip my pillow continuously to the cool side ("Come to the cool side, Luke!") and otherwise lay awake feeling like a sweathog if the temperature rises even a couple degrees above this threshold.

My wife, on the other hand, would fall asleep instantly in Hades (not that I believe she belongs there). They say that some like it hot, and she's definitely one of them.

So, after years of scientific study and scrupulous testing, we've arrived at a compromise that seems to work for us. First, we lower the temperature down to seventy degrees, which enables me to fall asleep beneath a mere sheet and blanket. Then, on the other side of our bed, my flannel-wearing wife burrows beneath a sheet, two blankets and an extra-large heating pad. Of course, this is our arrangement for summer; during the winter months, things can really get crazy.

Still, the plan tends to work okay, though sometimes when I'm feeling amorous I find myself rebuffed simply because I cannot locate my wife between all of those layers.

Another area where we differ is background noise. I prefer none. Just give me plenty of quiet and keep it coming.

Not surprisingly, my wife is partial to noise, especially talk radio. Tune in late night chit-chat and she immediately tunes out. The problem is, I can't help but listen to the conversations, regardless of how mind-numbing. Eventually, I find myself taking sides and, next thing you know, I'm calling the station to express my opinion.

"We have another caller on the line. Go ahead, caller."

"Okay. Well, I really think they should try to work it out. I understand why she got upset when she discovered he had a second wife up in Canada, but maybe that's just because he really cares about women."

I've also noticed that my wife and I fall asleep in completely different ways. Once she slides beneath all of her layers, she lies perfectly still until she passes into dreamland. Of course, the massive weight of the bedding likely has something to do with her immobility.

On the other side of the bed, I tend to move and adjust and twitch and roll until, like a restless canine, I find just the right sleeping position.

While I squirm, I am occasionally confronted by a muffled voice issuing the following command:

"Cut that out!"

To which I will promptly issue the standard male response:

"What?"

"Moving around," she will say, disregarding my innocent act. "I swear you've got bedtime A-D-D."

"I'm just trying to get comfortable," I will explain. "You want me to be comfortable, don't you?"

"Of course I do. In fact, I have just the thing to help you out."

Next thing you know, I'm stuck on my side, wrapped around my snoozing wife in the dreaded spooning position.

Yeah, well, I didn't need that arm anyway.

IS THERE A MIND-READER IN THE HOUSE?

This is not going to be easy, but I feel it is my duty as a purveyor of goodwill between the sexes to address a long-standing misconception. Women (and you know who you are), it is high time you realize the truth about us men: We are simple creatures, and we take what you say at face value.

I know you have suspected the "simple" part of this statement for some time now – say, from the moment you first saw us use the great outdoors as a bathroom or consciously slip on a pair of mismatched socks – but let me put to rest any doubts you may have: It's not an act.

We men are a guileless (and frequently clueless) fraternity. When you say something like, "Whatever you make for dinner will be fine," we believe you. As a result, we are flabbergasted when you berate us for serving you fish sticks and tater tots.

Apparently, you expect us to develop certain mind-reading capabilities as a result of taking our marriage vows. The reality is, we only become dumber.

As evidence of your unreasonable expectations, I cite a recent conversation I overheard between two women at a dinner party. One of the women explained to the other that she had instructed her husband not to buy her a Christmas gift that year, as they had already spent way too much money on gifts for their children.

Then she admitted that, "even though I said it, I will definitely hold it against him if he fails to buy me a gift."

As her friend nodded knowingly, she added that she would surely bring up "The Christmas You Never Got Me a Present" during every argument with her husband thereafter, until Kingdom come.

To this I say, "What gives?"

From a pragmatic viewpoint – yes, we men tend to be both simple and pragmatic – this kind of thinking might be considered counterproductive. Unfortunately, it also appears to be the rule in male-female relationships. Rather than telling us exactly what you want, or explaining exactly what you are thinking, you expect us men to figure it out for ourselves.

This is a supremely bad idea. If any of you women doubt me, I suggest you recall how your guy – without any direction – figured out for himself how to get to an unfamiliar destination the last time the two of you ended up lost in the car. Gives new meaning to the phrase, "Fashionably late," doesn't it?

Of course, it also leads to the following question: Why do women persist in playing these mind-reading games with their men?

I posed this question to my wife, and she responded with a one-word answer: "Romance."

Apparently, women find it romantic if their men can figure out what they want by some means (hypnosis and Sodium Pentothal come to mind) other than by simply coming right out and telling them.

Which brings me back to the fact that my brethren and I are too simple – too dense, really – to recognize the mysterious clues you provide us for solving these romantic riddles.

Oh, we will try and, occasionally, succeed; but more times than not, we will read your signals incorrectly or, like an anniversary date, miss them entirely. Inevitably, this leads to disappointment for you and the garbage disposal for a handful of innocent little fish sticks.

So, when my wife recently broached the subject of making New Years' resolutions, I suggested she vow to tell me what was on her mind, rather than making me guess.

"Do you really want me to do that?" she asked.

"Yes," I replied.

Then she took off the gloves and really let me have it.

This led me to quickly adjust my hypothesis: Sometimes, things are simply better off left unsaid.

A FINE MESS

When it comes to keeping my home office neat and organized, I am an abject failure. In fact, if organization is a sign of higher intelligence, scientists would take one look at my office and conclude it was the domain of a stressed-out houseplant.

Most of the time, I work under varying levels of disaster. Sort of like the Homeland Security Advisory System, which provides a color-coded warning of terrorist activity to the anxious American public.

Not too long ago, my wife raised the warning on my office from mauve ("sticky notes and pop cans on the loose") to chartreuse ("dangerously high stacks of paper about to tip over").

It's not that I am always a complete slob. My shirt is usually tucked in, and I generally shave every morning. I also clean the house, including the toilets, whenever the thought occurs to me. And, with two sons who apparently have better things to do than watch where they are aiming, cleaning the toilets is never a pleasant way to pass the time.

Me: "How the heck did you get so much pee on the shower curtains?"

Oldest son: "That's not my pee, it's his," he says, pointing in the direction of his brother.

Me: "Oh really? How can you be so sure?"

Oldest son: "Because he did it when I accidentally shoved him."

However, when it comes to my office, well, things can get pretty ugly.

Let's start with sticky notes, those little square pieces of paper with an adhesive back that come in multiple shapes, sizes and colors. My desk is covered with them. I will admit it here and now: I have a sticky-note problem. As soon as researchers come up with a patch that helps the wearer break the sticky-note habit, I'm going to give it a try. Heck, I might even sign up for one of those clinical trials.

The mass of sticky notes that are strung across my upright desk like a strand of Christmas lights contain names, phone numbers, germs of ideas, words of wisdom, reminders and to-do lists. In fact, the point of some of these sticky notes is to remind me of information contained on – yes – other sticky notes.

Things have gotten so bad, my wife gave me a fancy notebook with a thick, textured cover as a birthday gift.

"Keep it on your desk and jot down all your little notes in it," she suggested with all of the subtlety of a Mafia don. "Oh, and happy birthday."

Her plan was met with mixed success. If you open the notebook, the pages are filled all right – with many of my older, faded sticky notes. Those containing the newest information are back on my desk. I expect to find a dead fish on my chair any day now.

I also have a serious problem with pop cans. They decorate my table and shelves, and not in a good way. It seems I can leave my office for a few minutes and, when I return, they have secretly multiplied. Two cans will now be four, and four cans will now be eight. I have also made an interesting scientific discovery: Pop cans are hermaphroditic – a single can is capable of reproduction without the need of a sex partner.

Then there are my piles: Idea piles, bill piles, junkmail piles, magazine piles. The same year my wife gave me a notebook as a birthday gift, my in-laws bought me a paper shredder. I found it quite useful, actually.

The flat space on top was perfect for holding yet another pile of paper.

THE FOREIGN LAND NEXT DOOR

One Spring weekend, my wife and I traveled to a foreign country to attend a wedding. Only, this country was actually a nearby, Midwestern state.

Okay, so I exaggerated by using the "foreign" label. But only just a little.

You see, the residents of this state seem to follow strange or outdated customs, similar to what you might find when visiting a developing nation, such as Zambia or Canada.

For instance, a large segment of the population enjoys spending their weekends gathered together at RV camps. For the uninformed, an RV camp is any retention pond situated close by the interstate.

As my wife and I made the trip through this bizarre land early one Saturday morning, we noticed countless RV camps filling up with, well, RVs. The fact that it was fifty-five degrees and raining didn't seem to matter.

What they do at these places – with names such as Tiny's RV Park and Big Al's RV Oasis – is anyone's guess. Mine would be: Drink beer, eat pork rinds, play cards, talk about college football and drink beer. Then have the women folk rustle them up some breakfast.

After arriving safely at our destination, we entered the reception hall and appeared to step into a time warp set for 1985. The women sported big hair, the men wore mullets and cigarettes dangled from countless lips.

Then we noticed an armed policeman standing in the doorway. As the groom worked in law enforcement, we assumed the officer was just another guest.

Except he seemed to confiscate every envelope addressed to the bride and groom.

After questioning someone at our table, we discovered that the presence of the law was fairly typical at weddings in this locale. Apparently, receptions frequently dissolved into English soccer matches, with yelling and shoving and occasional fisticuffs.

What's more, we were told that having an officer present helped to ensure that the newlyweds' gifts didn't disappear during the reception.

Before we could seek out what we hoped would be complimentary bullet-proof vests, dinner was served. The family-style meal consisted of meat, with additional sides of meat, and a large bowl of beans. Everything was covered in gravy, including the defenseless beans.

A half-hour later, the dancing began.

Not that anyone moved all that quickly, laden as they were with a couple extra pounds of beef and beans.

Still, things managed to become quite festive. The bride and groom appeared completely in love, and the wedding guests enjoyed participating in a new-fangled line dance called The Hustle.

Then we heard a pair of loud voices.

Across the way, the bride's step-father was arguing with an older gentleman. My wife and I guessed that it had to do with hair – the step-father sported a ridiculous comb-over and the other fellow wore perhaps the worst toupee I had ever seen in public.

As their voices grew even louder, we discovered the issue had to do with Toupee's groping of Comb-over's wife while the two shared a dance.

Suddenly, they began to tussle, and Comb-over managed to put Toupee in a headlock. This also resulted in Toupee being displaced from his toupee.

Before you could clink a glass with your spoon, the police officer arrived to break up the wrestling match and escort Toupee, sans hair, out of the hall.

After that, folks resumed dancing as if nothing remarkable had taken place.

A little unnerved, my wife and I decided to call it a night and return to our hotel. We sought out the newlyweds and wished them good luck.

Based upon the way they stared into each other's eyes, I doubted they would really need it.

Then again, we heard that they were honeymooning at Big Al's RV Oasis.

Chapter Twenty-Five

PUSHING IT TO THE LIMIT

I've got a serious problem, and I'm sort of at a loss as to what to do about it. Therapy, electro-shock, a week of watching movies on the Lifetime channel – I'm not really sure the course to take.

This problem happens to be one of those uniquely-male quirks that drives women crazy, and not necessarily in a good way. More like in a yelling, name-calling, suspension-of-marital-relations sort of way.

You see, I enjoy running our car's gas gauge down to E, then coaxing it into the nearest gas station as the thirsty engine sucks up the last drop of petrol from the tank.

Of course my wife thinks I'm totally insane and isn't afraid to say so. Nor is she shy about her choice of adjectives in such moments. In fact, they tend to leave her mouth at a rate of speed that increases as the speed of our car decreases.

Why do I insist on playing this game? Is it some twisted form of male competition? Or, perhaps, could it be related to man's desire to conquer and control his environment?

I don't know, but what I do know is, it's been difficult to change my ways – especially now that we have entered an era in which automobiles come equipped with computer displays that keep a running tab on the exact number of miles left before empty.

No more eyeing the needle and guessing where E truly lies. Is it when the needle first hits the E or when it moves all the way through the E? Is it possible for the needle to move past the E and the car to still run? If so, does that trigger some sort of parallel universe in which the rules of physics no longer apply?

In today's automobiles, these intriguing questions no longer matter, as one glance at the display will tell you exactly how many miles until empty.

In fact, this happened during a recent family trip to the mall. As we pulled out of the driveway, my wife glanced at the computer reading.

"Ten miles till empty," she noted. "You better head right to a gas station."

"Oh, come on," I casually replied, "the mall is only five miles away. There's a bunch of gas stations right there."

"Do you have to do this every time?"

As I feigned innocence, we pulled up to a stoplight. The display registered eight miles remaining.

"Oh, great!" she exclaimed. "You used two miles worth of gas to go half a mile."

To annoy her even more, I gave the engine a couple of quick revs.

The reading suddenly slipped to seven miles. Oops.

As the light turned green and we started to move, I heard: "If we run out of gas, you're gonna wish this day never happened!"

"Come on, we're only four miles away," I countered. Still, I proceeded to push on the gas pedal gingerly, trying to conserve our precious supply.

We turned onto a back road leading to the mall. Only two miles away, but the reading had dipped to four miles left.

Less than a mile away, we pulled up to the final stoplight on our journey. The digital display told us we had two miles of gas left in the tank.

Then, as we sat there idling, the reading suddenly dropped to ZERO!

My wife and kids started screaming. It reminded me of that scene in the movie "Home Alone" when Macaulay Culkin slaps aftershave on his face.

Yet, when the light turned green and I lightly tapped the gas pedal, we began to move forward.

With beads of sweat dotting my forehead and my wife pounding my shoulder with her fist, I spotted a gas station up ahead.

Suddenly, the engine began to hesitate. In unison, all four of us leaned forward, as if this would magically bolster our momentum.

At this precise moment, the gas pedal went limp and we began to coast. I looked out the window and watched a dog trot past us.

Yet, all was not lost – the gas station was a mere hundred yards away!

Thanks to a stiff tail wind and an absence of on-coming traffic, we rolled slowly into the station, only to find every pump occupied.

A few minutes later, as I pushed our big SUV up to the pump beneath the evil glare of my wife and kids, I smiled a little smile, knowing I had taken it to the limit and survived to drive another day.

Chapter Twenty-Six

SAME YET DIFFERENT

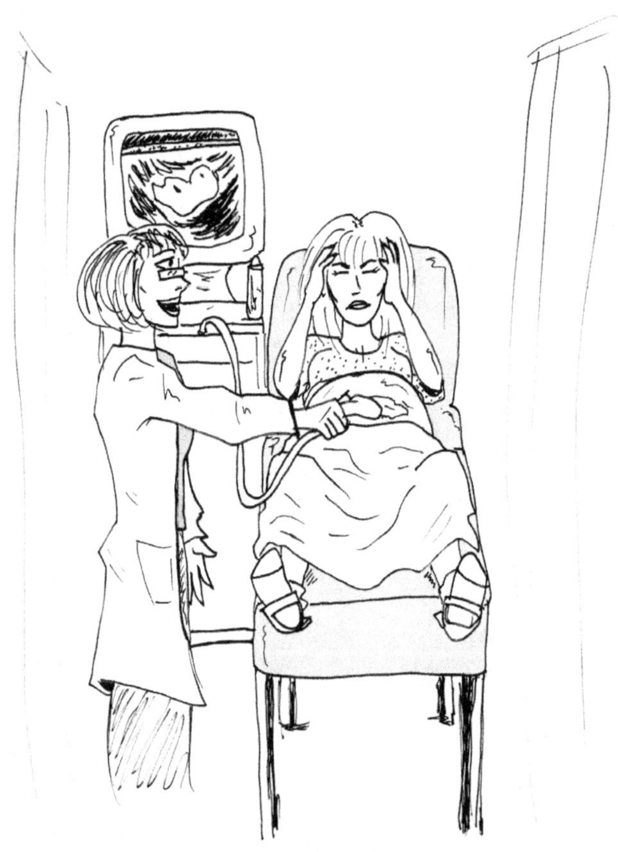

When I was fresh out of college and early into my first job as a reporter for a small town newspaper, I had the opportunity to interview a gregarious gypsy woman who made her living reading palms, deciphering tarot cards and communicating with the dead. After the interview, she offered to give me a reading "on the house."

Having very little to lose, I extended my hand and opened my mind.

She proceeded to cover a variety of topics concerning my future, but the thing that really got my attention was when she informed me that I would father five children during my lifetime.

All of them girls.

The funny thing is, I had always wanted to be the father of girls, as I had grown up in a family of all boys. Been there, done that. But girls were a mystery to me (some might say they still are), and I had always been drawn to the mysterious.

Years later, when we learned my lovely wife was in a family way for the first time, I was convinced I knew its sex.

"We're gonna have a girl," I declared, moments after completing my "I'm gonna be a father" dance.

"Why? Because of what that gypsy woman told you?" my skeptical wife replied.

"Uh-huh."

"You know that's a bunch of nonsense, right?"

Yet, when we had our first ultrasound and the tech asked if we wanted to know the sex of our baby, my rational wife shook her head and said, "I don't want to jinx it."

I turned to her a bit surprised. "You know that's a bunch of nonsense, right?" I said.

"Shut up," came her response.

And, so, we were both surprised when the baby came out a beautiful boy. Two years later, when we had a second boy, I started to get the distinct feeling that the gypsy woman might have been a fraud.

I also figured that my two boys would turn out to be quite similar in their interests and personalities. I couldn't have been more wrong.

Growing up, my oldest was your typical boy. He loved sports, rough-housing with his friends and breaking things apart, and he rarely paused for personal reflection. Meanwhile, my youngest was his brother's opposite in almost every way. He hated sports, disliked rough-housing and took to rebuilding each Lego creation his brother destroyed. He also was a deep thinker and, in many ways, what you might call an old soul.

Because I had coached my oldest in soccer, I signed his younger brother up for a team when he reached the minimum age. The first game, I sent him out for a shift as a field player. Moments later, he returned to the sideline.

"Can I come out, please?" he asked me.

"You just went in. Is something wrong?"

"Yes," he responded. "I don't like when I sweat."

When I sent him out for his next shift in the field, he proceeded to follow the referee around, asking him a variety of personal questions.

That would be his last shift as a soccer player.

We tried the slower sport of baseball, but the only thing that captured his interest was the young woman who, on Opening Day, walked out to the mound to sing the National Anthem.

Eventually, my wife and I discovered that our youngest son excelled in the performing arts. This led to piano lessons and theater classes. When he was eight years old, our youngest became the lead singer and keyboard player in a children's rock band, as well as the youngest performing member in a children's theater group. Like his brother with baseball and soccer, he had found his own niche.

We've never had any more children, and I've never, for a moment, regretted not having any girls.

Who could have predicted that?

Chapter Twenty-Seven

GOTTA HAVE THAT PIZZA PIE

It finally happened.

After years of health warnings concerning the foods we eat – red meat increases the risk of developing cancer, fish is filled with mercury, ice cream causes brain freezes – the dinner tables have finally turned.

I'm speaking, of course, of the announcement by Italian scientists that people who regularly gorge themselves on pizza – eating the equivalent of nearly two whole pies per week – experienced a significantly reduced incidence of certain cancers.

The news seems too good to be true. Sort of like that whole, bald is beautiful thing.

The researchers cited the antioxidant benefits of tomato sauce, the fiber content of dough and the nutrients in many of the toppings as a possible explanation for their findings. The fact that they happened to wear white chefs' hats with their lab coats should not discredit them in the least.

Indeed, I say these scientists gave a delicious new meaning to the word, "Ciao."

What's more, it is entirely possible this development is merely the tip of the iceberg lettuce. I suspect that the scientific community may soon announce that:

- Eating fried chicken dramatically improves one's eyesight;

- Gorging on mash potatoes and gravy increases one's flexibility;

- Chomping on chocolate bars drastically reduces the risk of gingivitis; and

- Regularly ingesting Chinese food not only heightens one's consciousness, it enables the eater to tell the fortune of perfect strangers.

Okay, that last one may be pushing it a bit. I couldn't help but become a little giddy, since pizza just happens to be one of my favorite meals. I love it in every shape known to man – round, square, deep dish, trapezoid – and in practically every variety – Dominos, Pizza Hut, Little Caesars, Hungry Howies, etc.

I eat pizza hot, cold, fresh and leftover. I scrape the cheese off the cardboard box and treat my sons' discarded crust as a delicacy.

Now, based upon Italian research, it actually turns out I'm not eating enough of it. This has got to be the greatest discovery since the microwave oven and Slurpies.

After hearing the good news, I immediately vowed to increase my family's pizza consumption by at least two pies per week. Of course, I knew I wouldn't get any argument from my sons. After all, they consider eating pizza their birthright.

It also occurred to me that the greater the amount of toppings decorating the pizza surface, the greater the health benefits. As a result, I further vowed to order my pies with more options than a new Mercedes. For the health benefits, of course.

As I was about to make a third vow concerning double cheese, my wife happened to walk by.

"Why are you so happy?" she inquired, suspicion dripping from her lips.

I showed her the news item.

"Interesting," she said as she read it.

I could see her wheels spinning. I considered engaging the brakes, but it was too late.

"So most of these test subjects lived their entire lives without getting cancer?"

"Yeah, so?" came my weak reply.

"Well, I bet eating all that pizza caused them to become grossly overweight, leading to heart disease, diabetes and other health problems. Of course, that would probably shorten their lives to the point where most of them died before they could come down with cancer."

Kaboom!

My hopes and dreams popped like a large mozzarella cheese bubble.

"You don't know that," I mumbled, but there was little conviction in my voice.

"Then go ahead – eat a pizza a day," she said, walking out of the room. "See if you can prove me wrong."

You know, I just might do that. Right after I buy me a pair of those pants with the elastic waist band.

CALL HER CINNAMON

While visiting the reading room recently, I found myself in a sticky predicament: None of my normal reading material was within arm's reach. No "Sports Illustrated," "Time Magazine" or local newspaper. Not even a Victoria's Secret catalogue. The only thing available was a copy of one of my wife's magazines – I think it was called "Cosmoglamourbook" – and I would rather read the label on a can of air freshener than a women's magazine.

"Honey," I called out, "can you bring me something to read?"

Hearing no response, I looked around for the air freshener, but it had disappeared. With no alternative, I succumbed to my need to read and picked up the Cosmoglamourbook. What can I say, I was desperate. Immediately, upon picking it up, I detected a flowery, perfumey odor that reminded me of the last time I was dragged into the Bath & Body Works store at the mall. Despite this affront to my senses, I started thumbing through the magazine.

I came across articles entitled "Love, Love, Love – Superglue Your Love" (sounded painful to me), "Sexier Sex" (or was it "Sexy Sex" or maybe "Sexier Sexy Sex," I don't quite remember) and something every guy would encourage - "52 Ways to be Even Sexier for Your Man." Now, like every red-blooded American male, I'm completely in favor of sexiness in women. But after a quick glance at some of the suggestions in this last article, I was left more dumbfounded than encouraged. For instance, "When you say something saucy to him in bed, do it in a pitch that's an octave lower than your usual talking voice."

I agree, assuming you want him to think he's about to have relations with a truck driver named Pat. Best case scenario, he thinks you're coming down with the flu and puts you in quarantine. Then there was, "Give yourself a special stripper name." I recommend either Delicious or Destiny. Or better yet, how about "Destiny Delicious." Hopefully, junior doesn't catch on and repeat mommy's new name for the kindergarten teacher. Of course, if a woman follows this suggestion, she also needs to be prepared to come home and discover her hubby has installed a stripper pole and trapeze in their bedroom. Along the same lines was the suggestion to "adopt a moving theme song." Just what every guy craves: Engaging in marital relations while Celine Dion belts out "My Heart Will Go On."

How about this suggestion: "Move in slow motion." That's right, act like you just dropped acid and woke up in a world where the atmosphere is maple syrup – a sure turn-on in my book. After all, what guy isn't attracted to a woman with the moves of an octogenarian pushing a walker? Then there was the seemingly innocuous suggestion to "eat dessert while staring into his eyes." Which, of course, should be immediately followed by the equally sexy "wipe the dessert off your chin." The final suggestion I read encouraged women to "create their own sex move." If you combine this with the stripper name and theme song, it might prove quite effective for launching that porn career you gals have secretly been dreaming about.

When I finished my business in the reading room, I walked into our bedroom to find my wife posed on the bed in some of her sexiest lingerie.

"Hey, sweety, what's going on?" I asked.

"Call me Cinnamon," she said in a husky voice.

NOT A LOTTO LUCK

I have never purchased a lottery ticket.

Now this may be hard to believe, what with all the hundred million dollar purses you keep hearing about, but I swear on a stack of bingo cards it's true. I just don't believe in it.

This caused a bit of an issue in our house when my wife decided to participate in the lottery club at work.

My reasons for abstaining are somewhat complex. You see, I have never been lucky – unlike some people who, it seems, happen to be born lucky. Take the Irish, for instance. They have a lucky mascot (the Leprechaun), a lucky cereal (Lucky Charms) and a lucky school (Notre Dame).

Or consider my cousin. If he puts on a pair of pants he hasn't worn in a while, he always finds money in the pockets. Once, he even found a twenty in a pair of pants he tried on at a local department store.

Me? I never find anything of value – unless a market suddenly springs up for lint balls, ticket stubs and gum wrappers.

When it comes to contests, I have never won anything of any substance. Not even a free taco at Taco Bell. But I'm okay with it. In fact, when the neighbors gather for poker night, I simply drop off a check and call it a night.

Because of my history with luck, however, I figure my odds of winning the lottery are actually higher than the average person. Call it

Murphy's Lotto Law. And winning the lottery is the last thing I want to do.

Why? Because I know what happens to the winners: Really bad things. I am a believer in the adage that money changes people. It changes the people that have it, and it changes the people around them that don't. The more the money, the greater the change. And these changes are rarely for the better.

Of course, if I were to win the lottery, I could simply give most of my winnings away. But this appears easier said than done. Lottery winners are bombarded with donation requests the moment their names surface in the public domain. Most requests are from reputable charities. Some are from Bob's Center for Cosmic Healing and Ten Minute Oil Change.

Then there's Uncle Al, who only needs a couple hundred thousand to get his synthetic rice farm up and running. Or Cousin Beth, who could use fifty grand to fund the launch of her picture-frame billboard business.

All worthy causes, but where does it end?

I haven't even touched on the changes that take place within the immediate family. I think I read somewhere that one lottery winner was sued by his son for a raise in his allowance, from ten dollars per week to a thousand dollars per week. Seems the boy suffered from a heavy candy habit. Ultimately, they settled out of court, but the damage was done.

Of course, my wife thinks I'm completely mental.

"We're not going to win," she told me when I decried her participation in the lottery club. "Besides, even if we did, the pot is split twenty-five ways, so we wouldn't end up mega-rich."

I quickly did the math in my head: $250 million pot divided by twenty-five winners, then reduced to present value on a lump-sum payout, minus taxes, probably resulted in a net figure of about one million dollars.

That was probably not enough to inflict severe damage upon our family unit.

But just about perfect to finance my dream of owning a center for cosmic healing and ten minute oil change.

Chapter Thirty

THE PANTS PUZZLE

When putting on a pair of pants, I always stick my left leg in first. Always. I had never given it much thought until the day my lovely wife happened to mention that people put their pants on the same way every time they dress – either left leg first, or right leg first.

At the time, we were enjoying our monthly date night at a local Italian restaurant.

"How do you know that?" I asked, slurping up my spaghetti.

"I read it in an online article," she replied, dodging flying specks of pasta sauce.

"Well, you shouldn't believe everything you read on the Internet," I noted.

"Okay, then, the next time you get dressed, try putting your opposite leg in first."

I started to unbuckle my belt.

"Not now," she said with a furrowed brow. "Wait until tomorrow morning."

Oh, right. That night I could barely sleep. Not one to shy away from a challenge, I kept visualizing what would happen the next morning when I attempted to put my pants on by starting with my right (or opposite) leg. I considered jumping out of bed right then and there to give it a shot, but I finally decided I should test the theory under optimum conditions. This meant conducting my experiment first thing in the morning, which is frequently the time of day that I put on some pants.

Though slightly sleep-deprived, the next morning I remembered the challenge the moment I rolled out of bed. Standing in our walk-in closet, pants in my hand, I told myself: "Right leg first...Right leg first." But the signal from my brain took a wrong turn, and next thing I knew I had my left foot up in the air. Either I was poised to insert it into my pants, or I was about to pee on a fire hydrant.

"Whoa!" I exclaimed.

"What is it?" inquired my wife from the bathroom.

"I almost put my left leg in my pants instead of my right."

"I'll alert the news media," came her reply.

Apparently, she had forgotten our dinner conversation. But instead of pointing this out to her, like a Zen master I focused all my concentration on my pants. See the pants, feel the pants, be the pants.

I lifted my right foot, held my pants open. Slowly, I forced my foot into the opening, then down into the right pant leg. Believe me, it wasn't easy. In fact, it actually felt like what I imagine an out-of-body experience to feel like. Still, a moment later my right foot popped out the bottom of the pant leg and hit the floor.

Success! Brimming with confidence, I proceeded to insert my left leg into my pants and immediately toppled over, hitting my head on a shelf in the process.

"What was that?" inquired my wife.

"I just fell down putting on my pants."

"Should I call nine-one-one?"

Once again I ignored her sarcasm to focus on the pants puzzle. Why was this task so difficult? Was it a right brain, left brain sort of thing? Are right-handed people predisposed to dressing left-leg first, and southpaws predisposed to doing the opposite?

Now, I'm not a psychiatrist, and I don't even play one on television, but I think it might have more to do with habit than anything else. After all, we human beings are creatures of habit. For instance, I tend to leave the toilet seat up after visiting the commode.

Do I do it intentionally, just to anger my wife? No. At least not most of the time. It's just one of my endearing little habits. In fact, I believe many of our habits serve a beneficial purpose. They provide us comfort, and even a little bit of sanity, during difficult or troubled times. Not that all habits are positive or beneficial. Take gambling, for instance. Or smoking. Or leaving the toilet seat up.

What does all this mean? Well, you're probably thinking that the way in which you put on your pants has little effect in the grand scheme of things.

But the large bump on my head would argue otherwise.

40 IS A LARGE NUMBER, BUT NOT AS LARGE AS 140

I had been moping around for weeks. Fortunately, I am an expert at hiding my feelings in order to minimize the impact on those around me.

"Would you stop leaving sticky notes with frowny faces around the house," ordered my understanding wife one day in the midst of my funk.

"Huh?" I responded.

"So, you're turning forty. It's not the end of the world."

"Easy for you to say," I declared. "You're only thirty-five."

"Hey – I'm thirty-four!" she barked. "My birthday is after yours. Is old age causing you to forget even the simplest of information?"

Ouch.

Yes, I was turning the ripe, old age of forty, and it was weighing on me like a three-hundred-pound lineman flopping on a fumbled football. In case you are wondering, in this scenario I am the football.

In my mind, I had passed life's halfway point and was now accelerating downhill toward the inevitable crash and burn of old age.

Ouch, indeed.

Fortunately, the next day we departed on a planned vacation at the celebrated wellspring of youth and cheer: Disney World in Orlando, Florida.

Although the trip was intended as a Christmas present for our boys, I figured it might also help me to get my mind off of the black cloud fixed over my head. Little did I know how true this would prove to be.

After we arrived at our hotel, my wife and children gleefully sprung a birthday surprise on me.

"We booked you a day at the Richard Petty Driving Experience," said my wife, handing me a brochure.

"It's part of Disney," said my younger son.

"Tomorrow, you get to drive a stock car," said my older son.

I responded with: "Huh?"

Now, I've never been a big fan of motor sports. And, despite my lead foot behind the wheel, I had never expressed an interest in driving a race car, stock or otherwise. So, while I eventually feigned excitement over the news, inside I was more than a little terrified.

The next day, we drove our rental car to the one-mile oval race track on the Disney grounds for my "experience." First, I joined the day's other participants in a small room to watch a video driving lesson. Next, we were fitted for jumpsuits and helmets, then boarded a cargo van for a guided trip around the track. This was followed by a ride in a stock car driven by a professional driver.

Finally, after pausing for photos with our families, we were given the opportunity to solo. This meant driving our own stock car as we followed a professional driver in his car. The more we demonstrated we could keep a proper distance and line behind the lead car, the faster he (and, therefore, we) would go.

Before you can say "Start your engines," I was averaging 125 mph around the track, including a top speed in the straightaways of 140 mph. And I was grinning the biggest grin that has ever graced my face.

"How was it?" my family asked after I climbed out of the car.

"Awesome!" I exclaimed.

"Pretty good birthday present, eh?" asked my older son.

"Whose birthday is it?" I replied.

The rest of the trip was a blur. I believe we met Mickey Mouse, ate dinner with Donald Duck, rode every ride in the park (twice) and watched multiple light parades.

The next week, I turned forty.

And the grin still hadn't left my face.

TIME TO MOVE

In the quest to find our personal version of Nirvana – that perfect combination of community, schools, neighborhood, house and lot – we moved to a quaint, little village on the outskirts of our big city.

And like any good quest, we endured our share of trials and tribulations.

The Trial of the Boxes.

To save a little money, we decided to move all of our boxed items, leaving only the items likely to cause a hernia for the moving company. During the four days between the closing and moving dates, we transported countless boxes to the new house.

Each night, I surveyed the boxes in our new home and smiled, knowing we had made a significant dent in the pile.

But each morning, I shockingly discovered the pile in our old home had managed to multiply, like a gaggle of rabbits ingesting Viagra.

Opening one of the boxes, I recoiled from a paper cut that nearly severed a finger.

"Yow!"

"What now?" came the emotionless response from my harried wife.

"I almost cut my finger off on the edge of this box!"

She examined the injury.

"It's just a tiny flesh wound," she proclaimed. "It's barely even bleeding."

"Easy for you to say," I replied, sucking on the wound.

My pain grew as I looked inside the offending box. It contained items that hadn't been unboxed since our last move, some five years before.

Or even longer.

"Dear?" I said using my thoughtful voice.

"What?"

"Do we really need this Oriental dinner set?"

"Yes. It was a wedding gift from a good friend of mine."

"But it hasn't been out of the box since our wedding night."

At this point, she opened a nearby box and pulled out a college text book.

"And what about your old Human Anatomy textbook?"

"What about it?"

"Hey, if you don't know your human anatomy by now..."

The Trial of the Well.

My wife and I were raised on city water. Cold, clear, chemically-altered city water.

Boy, did we miss it.

The water in our new house originated from a well. As in, a hole in the ground below our home. As a result, it tasted funny to us. But our water's worst quality was, without a doubt, the smell.

Actually, it reminded me of my childhood. And not in a good way.

One year, my mother forced us to hand-paint a bunch of hard-boiled eggs. Then, on Easter morning, my brother and I received orders to search for the eggs, as the Easter Bunny had hid them around the house during the night. This might have been fun, too, if not for the fact that I had begun shaving earlier that year.

Three months later, on an especially hot summer day, I began to detect an odor coming from behind our television cabinet. An odor so bad, it made me start to gag as I drew closer to it. An odor that seemed almost...inhuman.

Peeking behind the cabinet, I half-expected to discover a severed head. Instead, I spied a partially decomposed blob marked with a small skull and crossbones. During the time it took me to run to the bathroom and vomit, I realized the offensive odor originated from one of the Easter eggs I had painted.

The smell of our well water bore a striking resemblance to the Easter egg blob I had discovered almost thirty years before.

Our neighbors claimed we would get used to it. I think they were missing the point.

The Trial of the Cable.

The first two weeks after we moved, we had neither television nor internet service. The prior owners had used a satellite dish for the television and – gasp! – dial-up service for the internet.

As our family had no experience with a satellite dish – "Daddy, can we use it to contact aliens?" – and little desire to go from high-speed internet service to painfully-slow dial-up, we contacted the local cable company.

"Of course we can provide you with cable television and high-speed internet, sir. This is the new millennium."

Two weeks later, we were still stuck in the old millennium.

Meanwhile, my sons were on the verge of nervous breakdowns.

"Dad, if I have to watch this stinking video one more time, I'm gonna hunt down Sponge Bob and squeeze every last drop of water from his little yellow body!"

"Then how about playing a board game with your brother?" I suggested.

He looked at me like I was from another planet (summoned here by the satellite dish, no doubt).

"Fine" I said. "Let me see what I can do."

I located an ancient pair of rabbit ears and attached them to the one television in the house that was old enough to be compatible with them.

"What's that?" asked my boys.

"It's called an antenna. It's what we had to use to watch television when I was a kid. Before cable."

"So then it works without electricity?"

"Very funny."

I turned on the television and managed to locate a fuzzy show on ABC. It was either a professional bowling tournament or "The Wizard of Oz." All I could make out were a pair of red shoes.

My kids were so disgusted, they actually went to their room and began to read.

Eventually, we broke down and ordered satellite television and dial-up internet service. Life slowly began to take on some semblance of normalcy.

Meanwhile, my wife threatened me with great bodily harm should I ever again express a desire to move.

Which is a shame, really, since I discovered the backyard would not fit the in-ground pool I sort of had my eye on...

THE MORE, THE HAIRIER

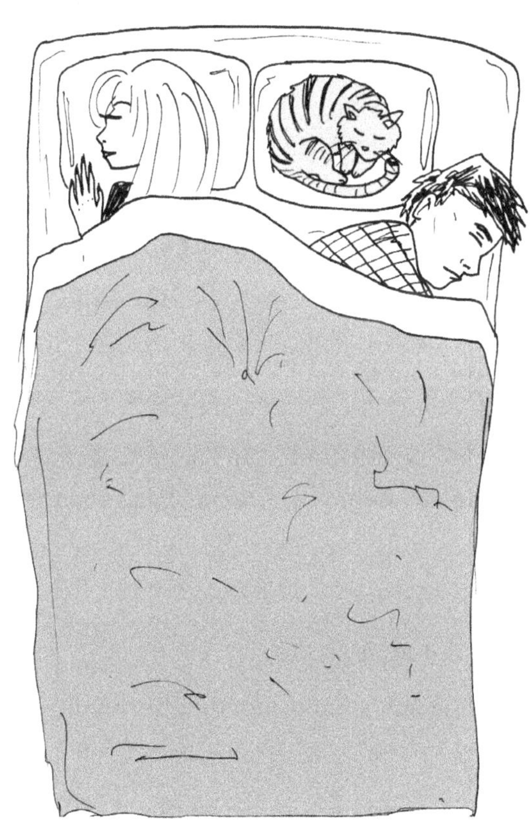

"Meow...Meow...MEOW!!!"

No, this isn't the transcript of a new cat food commercial, but rather a description of our morning alarm clock after my wife brought home an orphaned kitten from a nearby feed store.

I objected to the addition on the grounds that we already had a neurotic dog and irascible cat and why would we want to upset this delicate balance by throwing a new, and possibly more eccentric, personality into the mix? Not to mention the fact that kitty-litter duties always seemed to make it onto my chore list.

To no one's surprise but my own, this argument was quickly dismissed and our pet population swelled to seven, including the four remaining occupants of the science experiment known as my oldest son's fish tank.

The next big decision was its name. Resigned to the fact that the furry feline was probably here to stay, I figured we could at least give it a cool name – say, Artemis or Othello.

"Too pretentious," I was told.

Then how about something tough-sounding, like Spike or Nails?

"He's not the member of some grungy rock band," I was told.

When the cat hair settled, the new male member of the family was christened with the masculine moniker of...Mittens.

I'm sure the other cats in the neighborhood had a good laugh over that one.

Once named, Mittens-the-cat quickly climbed to the top of my "Things I Hate" list. He bullied our older cat, tormented our submissive dog and clawed our brand new furniture. Occasionally, he hacked up a furball the size of Vermont.

But these insolent acts were nothing compared to his habit of meowing outside our bedroom door at the first sounds of stirring in the morning.

Did I say "meowing"? I meant to say "MEOWING!!!"

You see, Mittens was always hungry, but he was especially hungry in the early hours of the morning. And, unwilling to wait until the human food-dispensers were fully awake, he would cry. And cry. AND CRY!

Not a sweet little kitten meow, either. No, his was a long, moaning, plaintive meow that went on for a good four or five seconds.

"MEEEEOOOOWWWW!!!"

Like a cat in need of an exorcist.

Or a new home.

This resulted in quite a predicament when, following a late night party at the neighbors, I awoke at 5:30 a.m. with an urge to visit the facilities.

What if Mittens heard me?

Like a burglar, I crept into the bathroom and slowly lowered myself onto the throne. Once finished, I encountered a new dilemma: To flush, or not to flush?

Crossing my fingers, I pushed down on the handle. Thirty seconds later: Nothing but silence.

With my mission a success, I crept back toward bed, knowing I had at least two more hours of soothing sleep ahead of me. Reaching my destination, eyes already closed, I stepped on a squeaky dog toy that lay on the floor like a devious trap.

"Squeak!"

"Son-of-a--"

"MEEEOOOWWW!"

Following a torrent of similar cries, my wife offered up a bit of standard female wisdom: "You woke him, you gotta feed him."

"But I never wanted the stupid cat!"

"Then why did you let us keep him?"

"What???"

"Go on. The food is in the pantry."

So, now you can understand why I hate the furry little creature. And as soon as he finishes taking his daily nap on my lap, I'm going to let him know it.

Chapter Thirty-Four

BF-GF, BUT ONLY FOR A MOMENT

My oldest son's twelfth birthday seemed to coincide with his discovery that girls were good for something more than serving as easy targets during gym-class dodgeball games. I couldn't have been prouder.

I had been waiting since his birth for the day to arrive when he would seek out my counsel regarding the opposite sex. I was really looking forward to imparting all the wisdom I had accumulated over the years, in hopes of making his journey into adulthood as smooth as possible.

Of course, my wife claimed that I would only need a few seconds to pass on all of my knowledge and experience, but what did she know?

"Don't you think you should just let him make his own mistakes?" she suggested.

"Why?" I responded. "So he can end up spending prom night in the basement watching reruns of 'Mash'?"

"Huh?"

"Never mind."

I proceeded to track down my son.

"Hey, got time for a little chat?" I asked.

"About what?"

"Well, I thought the two-of-us might talk about girls."

"Okay," he said. "What do you want to know?"

"Ha-ha," I replied, only to discover he was serious.

Apparently, kids were learning more at school than merely reading and writing, and my son was a major beneficiary of this "information sharing."

I quickly discovered that girls were just another subject he believed he knew everything about.

"You sure you don't want me to share my years of wisdom with you?"

"Thanks, Dad, but I think I'm good."

I guess I shouldn't have been surprised. I was exactly the same way when I was his age. Thought I knew it all and, what I didn't know, I could fake.

Of course, that only led to spending my prom night with Hawkeye and Trapper John.

A few weeks later, my son approached me with a pained look upon his face.

"Sup?" I asked, trying to sound cool.

"Nuttin'," came his reply.

"Really? You look sorta bummed out."

"Well, there's this girl I like, and she said she liked me. So I thought we were bf-gf (boyfriend-girlfriend), but then it turns out she was just using me to make some other guy jealous. So then he told her he liked her, and she dumped me."

"Huh..."

"How can someone be so mean?"

That's when I realized he still needed his old man. But it turned out that, instead of forcing my fatherly advice upon him, I simply needed to let him come to me.

I proceeded to tell him about the first time I experienced a broken heart and how, at the time, I didn't think I would ever get over it. Of course, I did get over it, and much sooner than I ever expected.

His mood seemed to brighten.

"You're gonna have lots of girlfriends before you finally settle down and get married," I told him. "And most of them will not be mean."

"I know," he said. "I've already got my eye on someone else."

"That's my boy," I said, patting him on the back.

With a little luck and a sprinkling of fatherly advice, there might actually be a prom in his future.

Chapter Thirty-Five

RUNNING ON EMPTY

Every year my small town holds a four-day summer festival to celebrate, well, summer. The events include an arts-and-crafts fair, a blind canoe race in which a blind-folded contestant paddles while a sighted contestant shouts out directions, a cold-butt euchre tournament in which contestants play cards while sitting atop blocks of ice, numerous musical acts and, most importantly, the ever-popular beer tent.

And every Sunday morning they hold a 5k running race. For you non-runners, this equates to 3.1 miles. I believe they offer this event to allow certain members of our community to sweat off the effects of the beer tent.

One summer, my then twelve-year-old son challenged me to run with him in the race. Not one to shrink from a challenge – I am a card-carrying member of the male sex, after all – I quickly agreed.

Now, like most men my age, I fancied myself as being in fairly good shape. I based this conclusion almost entirely upon the fact that the waist of my pants had only increased one size since graduating from college some twenty years before. Of course, the sad reality was, I hadn't run anything close to three miles in nearly an ice age. Meanwhile, my son was in his fifth year of competitive soccer and sometimes chose running over short trips in the car.

To play it safe, I bought some running shoes and decided to jog around town a few times before the event. This might have helped, too, if not for the fact that I kept stopping to talk with our neighbors – and anyone else who would listen.

Seeing my physical condition the day before the race, my wife offered some constructive advice.

"You know, you could always claim you pulled a muscle and drop out."

"Come on," I replied, "show a little faith."

"I would, if you could make it to the end of the driveway without pausing to rest."

"Hey, we've got an extra-long driveway," I reminded her. "Plus, I think there's a little slope to it."

At the starting line the next morning, I began to feel queasy, a condition which could likely be traced to a combination of pre-race jitters and a lengthy visit to the beer tent the night before. I looked around at my competition – middle-aged men with six percent body fat and the nerve to wear short-shorts – and began to sweat.

To calm myself, I focused upon a sure-fire plan: I would simply run with my son and ignore all of the other participants in the race. Maybe I could even give him a little push if he showed signs of slowing near the end.

This plan would quickly prove to be my downfall.

When the starter fired his pistol, my son took off like a sleek Italian sports car, eventually settling on a seven-minute-per-mile pace. My station-wagon body tried gamely to keep up, but I began to lose sight of him after the one mile mark. Even worse, the effort exerted in that first seven minute mile all but wiped me out, and I didn't make the two-mile mark until another ten minutes had elapsed.

From there, my pace dropped to something akin to a fast crawl. With alarms going off in various parts of my body and my thighs resembling two lifeless sides of beef, I concentrated on putting one foot in front of the other. I was determined not only to make it across the finish line, but to run the entire way.

A few moments later, I was passed by a woman pushing her twins in a stroller. As she jogged along, one of the twins looked back at me, perhaps curious to see what someone undergoing a near-death experience looked like.

Next came a rather obese fellow in tight, black biker shorts.

"Only a half-mile to go," he said encouragingly as he passed me by.

"Easy for you to say," I thought to myself. "You're probably motivated by that box of donuts waiting for you in your car."

A few agonizing minutes later, I saw it: A banner declaring the words, "Finish Line." Next to it was a large clock that read 29:22...29:23...29:24...

One hundred more feet and I could swear off running for the rest of my life.

That's when I heard them.

Two elderly women were coming up from behind, chit-chatting about their grandchildren. Worst of all, they weren't even running – they were fast-walking.

And so I made a momentous decision: I would salvage what little dignity I had left by beating these two grandmothers to the finish line.

I summoned my last bit of energy and picked up my pace, going from a fast crawl to a slow jog.

But so did my competition. They weren't going to let me have the satisfaction.

Soon, we were shoulder to shoulder.

I thought of throwing an elbow, but I was simply too exhausted to lift my arms that high.

Then they moved slightly ahead of me. You would have thought from the way they were motoring, a new widower had just arrived at the senior center.

With the finish line mere yards away, I somehow managed to semi-sprint and cross the finish line ahead of them, whereupon I promptly collapsed to the ground in a heaving heap of middle-aged flesh.

Laying there on my back, my chest rising and falling like King Kong after his fall to earth, I noticed the taste of victory in my mouth.

Between you and me, it tasted just like day-old beer.

THE MOLE HUNTER

Our current house occupies a large, wooded lot on the outskirts of a sleepy, little Midwestern village. Unlike the neighbors in our previous middle-class subdivision, no one really cares how the exterior of our house looks. I could plant a couple of rusted-out jalopies in our front yard, call them modern art and probably win an award from the village elders.

The problem is, I think my previous neighbors, with their lawn and landscape fetishes, may have rubbed off on me.

Recently, while mowing the lawn, I discovered an elevated trail running across a corner of the back yard, connecting one section of woods to another. The trail was about forty feet in length and even curved around our small koi pond. After doing a bit of research, I discovered our property had been invaded by a mole.

That evening, I informed the family of this outrageous new development.

"What do you plan to do?" asked my wife.

"What do you think? I'm gonna kill it."

"No!" screamed my younger son.

"Can't we keep it as a pet?" asked my oldest.

After I convinced my animal-loving family that a mole was not pet material, I headed for the hardware store.

My first attempt to eradicate the invader involved lighting what looked like a small stick of dynamite, dropping it into the mole tunnel and covering the hole with dirt. As I stood and watched, milky-white smoke seeped from various openings along the trail. I listened for the sounds of a rodent coughing, but none were detectable. Still, I had a good feeling about my efforts.

The next day I ventured into the back yard, only to discover the mole trail had been lengthened over night. Even worse, branches shot off the main line in a couple of areas, like off-ramps from a highway.

My second attempt to defeat my foe involved planting poisonous bait in various parts of the main trail. The bait looked like little rubber bugs and smelled like the sole of a thirty-year-old tennis shoe. Still, if they appealed to a mole, who was I to judge?

The next day I checked and discovered a couple of the deadly bugs had disappeared. This was a good sign. So was the fact that the trail had not changed in length or shape.

A few days later it was time to mow the lawn again. As I entered the back yard, to my horror I immediately noticed a number of new mole trails. Some were offshoots of the original line, some were in entirely different locations.

This was the last straw. I grabbed my garden hose, jammed it into the main line and turned the water on full. The little beast had better know how to swim...

Moments later, as large chunks of my yard disappeared below ground level and small pools sprung up where grass had previously grown, I sank to my knees, ready to admit defeat.

"What's wrong?" asked my wife from our nearby deck.

"I don't think I can win this battle," I said, dejection dripping from my lips.

"So that's it? You're just gonna quit? What happened to the man who didn't give up until I said 'Yes' to that stupid pony chair? The man who won't stop for gas until he sees zero miles left till empty? The man who refused to let two old women pass him during the last ten yards of running race? The man I married?"

She was right. I refused to let those octogenarians defeat me then, and I wouldn't let some beady-eyed rodent defeat me now.

A couple days later, after the furry devil had rebuilt his trails, I grabbed a chair, a couple magazines and a shovel and planted myself in the location of the most-recent activity along the mole highway.

Then I waited. And waited. And waited.

A couple hours later, as the sun was setting and I was about to call it a day, I saw it: Underground movement. The mole was digging away, extending his trail, no more than two feet from where I sat.

Like a ninja warrior, I grabbed my shovel and slowly rose to my feet. My breathing was even, my mind was focused.

I counted to ten in my head, then pounced!

Digging furiously in the location of the movement, I suddenly unearthed a small, hairy creature with a long, pointed nose and webbed feet.

The enemy was mine!

As it lay stunned on its back, I raised my shovel overhead and prepared to deliver the death blow.

"Stop!"

I turned to see my two boys running up to me.

"Don't kill it!" screamed my youngest with tears in his eyes.

"Have you seen what it's been doing to our yard?" I asked.

"It's one of God's creatures, Dad," injected my oldest.

The next thing I knew, the mole was scurrying about in a bucket as I walked it deep into the nearby woods.

The following week I noticed a fresh mole trail winding through my yard. But when I went to fetch my shovel, it was nowhere to be found.

THE DEVIL IN DISGUISE

There's a little devil loose in our house. This devil starts fights between family members, triggers mild anxiety attacks, likes to hide beneath seat cushions and generally causes more harm than good.

The devil I speak of is, of course, the television remote control. Or, in most homes, the "clicker."

A typical evening in our house goes something like this:

Older son: "Give me the clicker."

Younger son: "No. I was here first."

Older son: "Age before stupidity."

Younger son: "Actually, the stupid one says 'What?'"

Older son: "What?"

Younger son: "Ha!"

Older son: "That's it!"

As my older son chases his younger brother around the room, my wife enters.

Wife: "Stop it!"

After her offspring come to a halt:

"Now give me the clicker."

Younger son (handing it over): "But Maa-aam…"

Older son: "Nice work, bonehead."

Wife: "Don't call your brother names."

Older son: "What happened to freedom of speech?"

Wife: "The government made you that promise, not me."

Older son: "Man, this is so unfair!"

Me (entering the room): "Hi, Hon. Can I have the clicker, please? The game's about to start."

Wife: "Sorry. There's a new romance movie that I want to watch."

Me: "Man, this is so unfair!"

The funny thing is, my children don't realize there once was a time when you had to change television channels manually. Rise from your seated position, walk across the room, turn the knob, then return to your seat.

When I pointed this out to my boys, they looked at me like I was some sort of balding dinosaur. The fact is, I'm not sure today's televisions allow you to change channels manually, even if you are inclined to do so. Now, I'm not a scientist or health official, but perhaps this might account for the increase in obesity rates among our population.

Of course, with the advent of Tivo (or, in our house, DVR), your clicker now allows you to pause live TV, scroll backward and forward, and skip commercials altogether.

I envision a time when my grandchildren are watching television and their fathers (my sons) mention the old days, when all of the television shows shared time with commercials. Of course, this will be immediately followed by their children staring at them as if they are dinosaurs.

I only hope they aren't of the balding variety.

NAKED TWISTER

Apparently I was born 25-years too late. I say this because of some startling information I recently became privy to concerning the social lives of the modern day teenager. No, I'm not talking about hanging out at the local mall or spending one's allowance on lattes at Starbucks, but, rather, the boy-girl sleepover. For those parents out there who have yet to deal with zits, cell phones and speeding tickets, a boy-girl sleepover involves placing an equal number of boy teens and girl teens in one's basement, serving enough caffeinated pop and sugary treats to power a nuclear submarine, mixing in a handful of sleeping bags, then closing the door and going to bed. "Ha-ha," you're probably thinking, "you've obviously been sniffing Elmer's Glue again." After blowing my nose, my response to this is: I've got it on the best authority – the mouth of my newly-teenage son – that boy-girl sleepovers are all the rage in our suburban communities. It's an epidemic of Bieber-ish proportions.

I made this discovery recently when my oldest was invited to his first boy-girl sleepover at the home of one of his classmates. This led to a calm, rational discussion between my wife, my son and I.

"Can I go?" he asked.

"Let me see your voter registration card?" I responded.

"I don't have one."

"Then you can't go."

He quickly turned to his mother. "Maa-aam," he pleaded.

"Sorry," she said, "I don't make the rules."

My son and I responded with incredulous expressions.

"Okay, maybe I do make the rules," she admitted. "And, in this case, the rule is...no boy-girl sleepovers."

"That sucks!" he declared as he marched from the room.

"Can you believe that?" I said. "Holding a boy-girl sleepover with a group of teens is like handing a flamethrower to a pyromaniac – someone is bound to get burned."

"I don't know," responded my wife. "What if all of his friends are going?"

"So?"

"Do you really want him to be the only one who can't go?"

"Are you serious?" I said. "How about we just send him with a box of condoms. They can hand them out when they all play naked Twister."

"Now you're just being a smartass," she declared as she marched from the room.

As I stood there trying to figure out what had just happened, it occurred to me to call the host parents and give them a piece of my mind. I mean, what possible good could come from a boy-girl sleepover? Improving teenage communication skills? Yeah, they'll all be speaking in tongues before the night's over. Encouraging the participants to get out of their comfort zones? Yeah, they'll get so far out, half the sleeping bags will go unused. The situation had the makings of a new reality TV show. Call it, "The

Mating Rituals of the Modern American Teen." Asking teenagers to be good under such circumstances is like asking Republicans and Democrats to play nice – it sounds good in theory, but it never works in practice.

Back when I was a teen, the closest I ever came to a boy-girl sleepover was when I had a few of my guy friends spend the night and one of them pulled out a bootleg copy of Playboy. Unfortunately, the party went straight downhill after that. We had to kick one of the guys out for suggesting we play truth-or-dare, and another excused himself after realizing he had forgotten his inhaler. That left only two of us – an awkward number for an all-male sleepover – so we spent the rest of the night at opposite ends of the room.

Now, some 25-years later, I had learned it's acceptable to invite the opposite sex to such an affair. Well, the first thought crossing my mind was, it won't be happening on my watch.

Followed quickly by a second thought: Anyone up for a quick game of naked Twister?

ARE WE THERE YET?

Are we there yet?

This well-known phrase can have more than one application.

Of course, the most common of these is serving as the annoying question that is posed repeatedly by underage passengers in the rear of a vehicle during any journey lasting longer than it takes to travel the length of one's driveway.

My youngest son is a frequent perpetrator of this moving violation. In fact, his habit had become so annoying, I took him aside a few days before our last driving vacation and laid down the law.

"Can you do me a really big favor on this vacation?"

"You want me to drive?" he asked.

"No, funny guy, I want you to try your hardest not to ask me 'Are we there yet?' during the trip."

"I can do that," he promised.

Later that week, as we motored along the interstate under clear, blue skies, a voice behind me called out: ¿ya llegamos?

Yes, he had taught himself how to say 'Are we there yet?' in Spanish.

This phrase can also apply to that point in time in which one's children have grown and the nest becomes officially empty, save for the pitter-patter of spousal feet.

If I were to answer this question with respect to my own particular family unit, my answer would be, "Half way." As I am writing this, I have been happily married for fifteen years and my two sons are the ripe old age of eleven and thirteen. Another seven years or so, and the nest should once again belong to the two of us.

It has been a fun ride so far. With any luck at all, I'll check back in with you when I can answer the question, "Are we there yet?" with a "Yes."

Marc L. Prey is an award-winning screenwriter with more than a dozen film and television credits. He is also an internationally-produced playwright and the published author of short fiction, nonfiction, essays and humor. In his spare time, he teaches screenwriting at a local film school and chases after his dog, Buddy. Born and raised in Michigan, Marc takes his Midwestern values with him wherever he travels.